Francis Frith's
LINCOLNSHIRE

PHOTOGRAPHIC MEMORIES

Francis Frith's
LINCOLNSHIRE

◆

Martin Andrew

First published in the United Kingdom in 2000 by
Frith Book Company Ltd

Hardback Edition 2000
ISBN 1-85937-135-3

Paperback Edition 2001
ISBN 1-85937-433-6

Reprinted in Hardback 2001

Reprinted in Paperback 2003

British Library Cataloguing in Publication Data

Francis Frith's Lincolnshire
Martin Andrew

Frith Book Company Ltd
Frith's Barn, Teffont,
Salisbury, Wiltshire SP3 5QP
Tel: +44 (0) 1722 716 376
Email: info@francisfrith.co.uk
www.francisfrith.co.uk

Printed and bound in Great Britain

Contents

Francis Frith: Victorian Pioneer   7

Frith's Archive - A Unique Legacy   10

Lincolnshire - An Introduction   12

The North: The Kingdom of Lindsey:
Gainsborough to Horncastle   18

Around Lincoln   36

The South West: Grantham & Kesteven   50

The South East: Boston & The Flat Country
of Holland   74

Seaside Lincolnshire   98

Index   115

Free Mounted Print Voucher   *119*

◆

FRANCIS FRITH: *Victorian Pioneer*

FRANCIS FRITH, Victorian founder of the world-famous photographic archive, was a complex and fascinating man. A devout Quaker and a highly successful Victorian businessman, he was both philosophic by nature and pioneering in outlook.

By 1855 Francis Frith had already established a wholesale grocery business in Liverpool, and sold it for the astonishing sum of £200,000, which is the equivalent today of over £15,000,000. Now a multi-millionaire, he was able to indulge his passion for travel. As a child he had pored over travel books written by early explorers, and his fancy and imagination had been stirred by family holidays to the sublime mountain regions of Wales and Scotland. 'What a land of spirit-stirring and enriching scenes and places!' he had written. He was to return to these scenes of grandeur in later years to 'recapture the thousands of vivid and tender memories', but with a different purpose. Now in his thirties, and captivated by the new science of photography, Frith set out on a series of pioneering journeys to the Nile regions that occupied him from 1856 until 1860.

INTRIGUE AND ADVENTURE

He took with him on his travels a specially-designed wicker carriage that acted as both dark-room and sleeping chamber. These far-flung journeys were packed with intrigue and adventure. In his life story, written when he was sixty-three, Frith tells of being held captive by bandits, and of fighting 'an awful midnight battle to the very point of surrender with a deadly pack of hungry, wild dogs'. Sporting flowing Arab costume, Frith arrived at Akaba by camel seventy years before Lawrence, where he encountered 'desert princes and rival sheikhs, blazing with jewel-hilted swords'.

During these extraordinary adventures he was assiduously exploring the desert regions bordering the Nile and patiently recording the antiquities and peoples with his camera. He was the first photographer to venture beyond the sixth cataract. Africa was still the mysterious 'Dark Continent', and Stanley and Livingstone's historic meeting was a decade into the future. The conditions for picture taking confound belief. He laboured for hours in his wicker dark-room in the sweltering heat of the desert, while the volatile chemicals fizzed dangerously in their trays. Often he was forced to work in remote tombs and caves where conditions were cooler. Back in London he exhibited his photographs and was 'rapturously cheered' by members of the Royal Society. His reputation as a photographer was made overnight. An eminent modern historian has likened their impact on the population of the time to that on our own generation of the first photographs taken on the surface of the moon.

VENTURE OF A LIFE-TIME

Characteristically, Frith quickly spotted the opportunity to create a new business as a specialist publisher of photographs. He lived in an era of immense and sometimes violent change. For the poor in the early part of Victoria's reign work was a drudge and the hours long, and people had precious little free time to enjoy themselves.

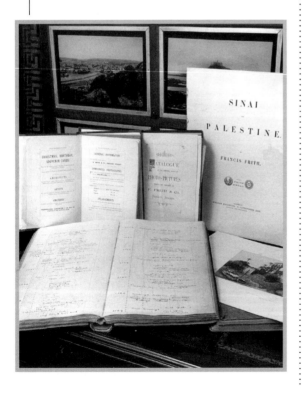

Most had no transport other than a cart or gig at their disposal, and had not travelled far beyond the boundaries of their own town or village. However, by the 1870s, the railways had threaded their way across the country, and Bank Holidays and half-day Saturdays had been made obligatory by Act of Parliament. All of a sudden the ordinary working man and his family were able to enjoy days out and see a little more of the world.

With characteristic business acumen, Francis Frith foresaw that these new tourists would enjoy having souvenirs to commemorate their days out. In 1860 he married Mary Ann Rosling and set out with the intention of photographing every city, town and village in Britain. For the next thirty years he travelled the country by train and by pony and trap, producing fine photographs of seaside resorts and beauty spots that were keenly bought by millions of Victorians. These prints were painstakingly pasted into family albums and pored over during the dark nights of winter, rekindling precious memories of summer excursions.

THE RISE OF FRITH & CO

Frith's studio was soon supplying retail shops all over the country. To meet the demand he gathered about him a small team of photographers, and published the work of independent artist-photographers of the calibre of Roger Fenton and Francis Bedford. In order to gain some understanding of the scale of Frith's business one only has to look at the catalogue issued by Frith & Co in 1886: it runs to some 670

pages, listing not only many thousands of views of the British Isles but also many photographs of most European countries, and China, Japan, the USA and Canada – note the sample page shown above from the hand-written *Frith & Co* ledgers detailing pictures taken. By 1890 Frith had created the greatest specialist photographic publishing company in the world, with over 2,000 outlets – more than the combined number that Boots and WH Smith have today! The picture on the right shows the *Frith & Co* display board at Ingleton in the Yorkshire Dales. Beautifully constructed with mahogany frame and gilt inserts, it could display up to a dozen local scenes.

POSTCARD BONANZA
◆◆

The ever-popular holiday postcard we know today took many years to develop. In 1870 the Post Office issued the first plain cards, with a pre-printed stamp on one face. In 1894 they allowed other publishers' cards to be sent through the mail with an attached adhesive halfpenny stamp. Demand grew rapidly, and in 1895 a new size of postcard was permitted called the

court card, but there was little room for illustration. In 1899, a year after Frith's death, a new card measuring 5.5 x 3.5 inches became the standard format, but it was not until 1902 that the divided back came into being, with address and message on one face and a full-size illustration on the other. *Frith & Co* were in the vanguard of postcard development, and Frith's sons Eustace and Cyril continued their father's monumental task, expanding the number of views offered to the public and recording more and more places in Britain, as the coasts and countryside were opened up to mass travel.

Francis Frith died in 1898 at his villa in Cannes, his great project still growing. The archive he created continued in business for another seventy years. By 1970 it contained over a third of a million pictures of 7,000 cities, towns and villages. The massive photographic record Frith has left to us stands as a living monument to a special and very remarkable man.

Frith's Archive: *A Unique Legacy*

FRANCIS FRITH'S legacy to us today is of immense significance and value, for the magnificent archive of evocative photographs he created provides a unique record of change in 7,000 cities, towns and villages throughout Britain over a century and more. Frith and his fellow studio photographers revisited locations many times down the years to update their views, compiling for us an enthralling and colourful pageant of British life and character.

We tend to think of Frith's sepia views of Britain as nostalgic, for most of us use them to conjure up memories of places in our own lives with which we have family associations. It often makes us forget that to Francis Frith they were records of daily life as it was actually being lived in the cities, towns and villages of his day. The Victorian age was one of great and often bewildering change for ordinary people, and though the pictures evoke an impression of slower times, life was as busy and hectic as it is today.

We are fortunate that Frith was a photographer of the people, dedicated to recording the minutiae of everyday life. For it is this sheer wealth of visual data, the painstaking chronicle of changes in dress, transport, street layouts, buildings, housing, engineering and landscape that captivates us so much today. His remarkable images offer us a powerful link with the past and with the lives of our ancestors.

TODAY'S TECHNOLOGY

Computers have now made it possible for Frith's many thousands of images to be accessed almost instantly. In the Frith archive today, each photograph is carefully 'digitised' then stored on a CD Rom. Frith archivists can locate a single photograph amongst thousands within seconds. Views can be catalogued and sorted under a variety of categories of place and content to the immediate benefit of researchers. Inexpensive reference prints can be created for them at the touch of a mouse button, and a wide range of books and other printed materials assembled and published for a wider, more general readership. The day-to-day workings of the archive are very different from how they were in Francis Frith's

See Frith at www.francisfrith.co.uk

time: imagine the herculean task of sorting through eleven tons of glass negatives as Frith had to do to locate a particular sequence of pictures! Yet the archive still prides itself on maintaining the same high standards of excellence laid down by Francis Frith, including the painstaking cataloguing and indexing of every view.

It is curious to reflect on how the internet now allows researchers in America and elsewhere greater instant access to the archive than Frith himself ever enjoyed. Many thousands of individual views can be called up on screen within seconds on one of the Frith internet sites, enabling people living continents away to revisit the streets of their ancestral home town, or view places in Britain where they have enjoyed holidays. Many overseas researchers welcome the chance to view special theme selections, such as transport, sports, costume and ancient monuments.

We are certain that Francis Frith would have heartily approved of these modern developments, for he himself was always working at the very limits of Victorian photographic technology.

THE VALUE OF THE ARCHIVE TODAY

Because of the benefits brought by the computer, Frith's images are increasingly studied by social historians, by researchers into genealogy and ancestory, by architects, town planners, and by teachers and school-children involved in local history projects. In addition, the archive offers every one of us a unique opportunity to examine the places where we and our families have lived

and worked down the years. Immensely successful in Frith's own era, the archive is now, a century and more on, entering a new phase of popularity.

THE PAST IN TUNE WITH THE FUTURE

Historians consider the Francis Frith Collection to be of prime national importance. It is the only archive of its kind remaining in private ownership and has been valued at a million pounds. However, this figure is now rapidly increasing as digital technology enables more and more people around the world to enjoy its benefits.

Francis Frith's archive is now housed in an historic timber barn in the beautiful village of Teffont in Wiltshire. Its founder would not recognize the archive office as it is today. In place of the many thousands of dusty boxes containing glass plate negatives and an all-pervading odour of photographic chemicals, there are now ranks of computer screens. He would be amazed to watch his images travelling round the world at unimaginable speeds through network and internet lines.

The archive's future is both bright and exciting. Francis Frith, with his unshakeable belief in making photographs available to the greatest number of people, would undoubtedly approve of what is being done today with his lifetime's work. His photographs, depicting our shared past, are now bringing pleasure and enlightenment to millions around the world a century and more after his death.

LINCOLNSHIRE – *An Introduction*

IF YOU TALK about Lincolnshire to people, as I often do (my mother was born and brought up in Gainsborough and many of my holidays were spent there in the 1950s), the flatness of the county will be the first thing mentioned. Indeed, parts of the county are flat, particularly in the south-east, in the parts of Holland bordering on the Wash. But this is not the whole picture: much of the county is rolling limestone country reaching nearly 500 feet above sea level in the south-west in the parts of Kesteven around Stamford and Grantham, with a limestone ridge running north of Lincoln to the banks of the River Humber. Further east are the Wolds, expansive chalk uplands with oceans of wheat and barley and deep-cut winding river valleys, such as those cut by the River Lymn north-west of Spilsby. These rise to over 550 feet.

Admittedly the whole of the south-east of the county is almost unrelievedly flat, with drains, dykes and canalised rivers and settlements along banks or on knolls that rise a mere few feet above the surrounding drained marshes or fens. This produces vast skies with towering clouds and long views of the higher land beyond, and the buildings thus assume greater significance. Who can forget their first long views of Lincoln Minster's three great towers atop the limestone ridge where the River Witham cuts through it, the setting sun bathing the towers and the clouds in roseate light, or the Boston Stump, that sublime church steeple, seen from the Spalding direction, or even Tattershall Castle's mighty medieval brick keep?

Amidst this great variety of landscapes are set a remarkable number of small market towns, such as Horncastle, Bourne, Spilsby and Holbeach, and small villages of every style and layout, from those such as brick-built Sutton St James that follow a dyke-top road, to warm golden oolitic limestone villages in the south-west on the edge of the Vale of Belvoir, such as Skillington. Apart from the magnificent county town of Lincoln, there are fine large towns, such as the coaching towns of Grantham and Stamford, the latter a stone-built town of the highest quality and completeness, or Boston, Louth and Spalding. There are other areas of flat country, such as the valley of the River Trent and the clay vale between the limestone ridge and the Wolds, and east of the Wolds between them and the sand-dunes of the North Sea coast. To a Lincolnshireman, the flat land only serves to make the high ground more effective. Certainly the western scarp of the Lincoln Cliff, as the limestone ridge is known north of Lincoln, or of the Lincoln Edge, as it known south of Lincoln as far south as Welbourn, is spectacularly steep; its 200 to 300 feet seem remarkably high, while from the ridge the views are vast across the Vale of Trent to the west.

As ever, the character of a county comes partly from the range of building materials from which it is forged and wrought. Lincolnshire is no exception: its character varies from the stoneless fens, where brick predominates, to the glorious stones of the south-west, the best of which is the Ancaster stone, which was widely exported for the best buildings in England. Rougher limestones are common; the stone villages extend wherever the limestone is found, such as Hemswell, east of Gainsborough. On the edge of the Wolds are greensands (often brown, rather than green), Spilsby sandstone and some chalk-stone; but brick is perhaps the building material of the bulk of the county, from the great medieval buildings such as Tattershall Castle, Wainfleet School or the lodgings range of Gainsborough's Old Hall, down to the artisan and workers' terraces of Lincoln south of the Witham. Even a town like Grantham, on the limestone, used brick for its Georgian town houses, despite being in stone country. Timber-framing is relatively uncommon, and 'mud and stud' cottages are now distinctly rare (a light timber frame with mud walls). Unfortunately, there has been a depressing recent trend to render a lot of Lincolnshire's brick with modern 'never decorate your

house again' wondercoatings, and huge numbers of older windows have been replaced by either nasty 1960s timber ones or that modern seducer of character, the plastic window.

History in Lincolnshire makes its presence felt for the first time after the Roman conquest in 43 AD. What is now Lincoln was established as a legionary fortress around 47 AD, for its strategic value was obvious to the Romans. The history of Lincoln itself and its transformation into 'Lindum Colonia', elided into Lincoln later on, can be found in my introduction to the companion Francis Frith Collection book 'Around Lincoln'. For the rest of what is now Lincolnshire, the Roman impact was profound: Ermine Street (not a Roman name of course) ran through the county from Stamford, where it crossed the River Well, and on to Winteringham on the River Humber, where it crossed by ferry to continue on to York. The Fosse Way, which runs from Axminster to Lincoln, enters the county north-east of Newark to merge with Ermine Street south of the city. There are other Roman roads, including King Street, which runs from Peterborough to Lincoln via Bourne, while various roads head east from Ermine Street onto and across The Wolds, one as far as Burgh le Marsh, which was then on the coast. Other important roads include the one from near Bourne into the marshes, which in Roman times were important salt-producing areas; it then headed north-west from Lincoln to cross the Trent at Littleborough, heading for Doncaster.

Besides the roads, the Romans undertook some mighty engineering works which were not equalled until Vermuyden and his Dutch compatriots in the 17th century drained the fens and the Isle of Axholme. These include

Foss Dyke, a canal still in use, that linked Lincoln to the River Trent, the Sincil Dyke, and above all the Carr Dyke. This last was a banked canal dug after 120 AD to collect clearly visible, while Lincoln was, of course, a walled town; part of its north gate, the Newport Arch, survives intact.

After the end of Roman occupation, the

SKEGNESS, GRAND PARADE 1910 62845

flood water and the rivers and streams flowing from higher ground so as to prevent flooding of the fenland. It runs from the Witham, three miles south of Lincoln, for 56 miles as far south as the River Nene, and long stretches still carry water even now. Further out the Romans embanked the coast: the road names Roman Bank in Skegness and Chapel St Leonards relate to this prodigious activity. Caistor, Ancaster and Horncastle were walled towns; stretches of Caistor's walls have been recovered by excavation, while parts of Horncastle's remain above ground. Ancaster, just north of the junction of King and Ermine Streets, has its southern earthwork defences

Anglo-Saxon conquerors did little reclamation in the fens and lowland marshes, but Lincolnshire became a political entity for the first time as the Anglian Kingdom of Lindsey. The genealogy of the kings survives, and the area it covered fluctuated, with the present area of the former county of Lindsey its heartland. The kingdom was absorbed by Mercia not long after 700 AD, but it says much for the historical awareness of the area's traditions that when Lincolnshire emerged into the daylight of Domesday Book after the turmoil of the Danish era, the north part of the county had the name of Lindsey. It had been absorbed into the Danish colonised area, and was further sub-divided into three parts, the West, North and South Treding, the Danish word for 'third thing', thing being a council or assembly, just like Yorkshire with its Ridings or thirds. Also in Domesday Book, the south-west of the county has its own administrative area, Chetsteven, now spelt Kesteven, and Holland is also distinguishable.

This all demonstrates a remarkable historic continuity from the Anglo-Saxon to the Norman period. According to the Anglo-Saxon Chronicles, in 627 AD Lindsey was converted to Christianity by Paulinus, although it only got its first bishop in 678 AD, one Eadhed. Being on the east coast, and with the Trent and Witham highly navigable, the then Mercian province of Lindsey was highly vulnerable to the longship-borne marauding armies of Danes, who are first recorded in the Chronicles as ravaging the area in 839 AD. Subsequently there was considerable Danish settlement: hundreds of Danish place names can be found, particularly in the northern two-thirds of Lincolnshire. Place names ending in -by, -toft, -thorpe, and -ness, for example, abound; these include Stragglethorpe (a wonderfully ugly name), Ulceby, Wigtoft and Skegness. After Guthrum's peace with Alfred the Great in 886 AD which created the Danelaw, the whole of eastern Mercia, including its province of Lindsey, was ruled by armies based in the Five Boroughs: Stamford and Lincoln were two of them, Derby, Leicester and Nottingham the other three. Although Lincolnshire was reconquered by the English by 920AD, the Danish left an indelible imprint, together with large numbers of settlers who changed the ethnic mix for ever. Indeed, in 1013-14 Gainsborough was England's capital - Sweyn Forkbeard

received the submission of the English rulers here. Sweyn died in Gainsborough on 2 February 1014 and his son, the famous King Canute, subsequently ruled England.

Lindsey's last reference in the Anglo-Saxon Chronicles ushers in a new era: in 1066, it reports that Earl Tostig, King Harold's brother, harried Lindsey and killed many good men there. Later Harold died at the Battle of Hastings, and England was conquered by William the Conqueror, Duke of Normandy. Before the Conquest there had been some major stone building, none more impressive than the minster church at Stow north-west of Lincoln, and there are many smaller churches with notable work, such as Barton-on-Humber, Hough on the Hill, Scartho and Broughton. But after the Conquest there was a great outburst of building, not only in Lincolnshire of course; but there are quite exceptionally important Norman buildings in the county. These range from the mighty westwork of Lincoln Minster or Cathedral (the seat of Remigius' bishopric transferred from far-away Dorchester on Thames), the so-called Jews' Houses in the city and St Mary's Guildhall to its south, to Boothby Pagnell manor house. Besides these crucial buildings for students of architectural history, there are numerous churches with Norman work, such as the chancel of Stow, fragments at Crowland Abbey, St Leonards Priory at Stamford and parish churches such as Whaplode or Sempringham.

The high Middle Ages were centuries of great wealth for Lincolnshire, based to a great extent on wool, and this funded some outstanding architecture. Who can forget the magnificent well-nigh architecturally perfect Boston Stump, a 15th-century tower with an early 16th-century lantern atop its 272 feet, Louth's roughly contemporary west tower and spire, totalling 295 feet in height, or Grantham's much earlier (13th-century) tower and spire 282 feet high? But these pale into insignificance beside Lincoln Minster's superlative Gothic work crowned by the sublime central and west towers; these can be seen from miles around and symbolise the importance of the city to the county. The list is long, and no-one who loves medieval churches could possibly by-pass Lincolnshire. All this reflected great wealth, and indeed the port of Boston, a new town planted around 1100, was paying more customs duties than London itself by the late 13th century. A late flowering of medieval architecture produced some superb brick buildings in areas where stone for building was rare. These include Tattershall Castle of the 1430s, Hussey's Tower in Boston, the Wainfleet School of 1484 and the 15th-century lodging ranges and tower of Gainsborough's Old Hall. For architectural heritage purposes, the decline of the county into an economic backwater with the demise of the wool trade in Tudor times preserved much more of its medieval heritage than continued economic success would have done.

By 1600 much of the county's wealth resided in agriculture, with the numerous market towns being the trade centres for their hinterlands. Great country houses replaced the abbeys, such as Thornton and Crowland, as the gentry and squirearchy built and rebuilt. Doddington Hall, Belton House,

SKEGNESS, LUMLEY ROAD 1899 44354

Gunby Hall, Grimsthorpe Castle, Culverthorpe Hall, Fillingham Castle and Harlaxton are a few of the survivors. Others were lost in the great country house Demolition Derby after World War II, including Bayons Manor and Tupholme Hall.

Not all Lincolnshire was agrarian, although many industries were based on agricultural products, such as the vast Maltings at Sleaford. Grimsby grew from a declined medieval port into the fifth largest in England after a new dock was built in 1800; this was followed by the arrival of the railway in 1848, and further docks came in the 1850s, including a major fish dock for the trawler fleet. Many highly advanced windmills survive, dating from the early 19th century, while brewing and malting were natural industries for such a rich agricultural county. However, only Bateman's of Wainfleet still brews. Other towns specialised in agricultural machinery, including Gainsborough, which diversified into packaging machinery. My grandfather, Wilfred Durdey, was joint managing director of Rose Brothers in Gainsborough, whose wrapping machinery was sold world-wide. Grantham saw the first mass-produced diesel engines built in Hornsby's factory, and Lincoln had Smith's Crisps, among other industries, until the factory burned down.

On the east coast, the long sandy beaches beyond the sand dunes were seen to have potential for seaside resort development; the arrival of the railways from the Midlands in the second half of the 19th century led to their rapid, some might say under-regulated, development and their flooding with Midland day-trippers arriving by railway. Skegness started off as genteel while the Earl of Scarbrough was in control, but it soon headed for the lower end of the market. A whole string of seaside resorts grew up, from Cleethorpes in the north to Skegness via Mablethorpe, Sutton on Sea, Chapel St Leonards and Ingoldmells. Butlins built its first holiday camp at Ingoldmells in 1936, and nowadays there are vast arrays of caravan sites, amusement arcades, fun fairs and cafes to cater for trippers visiting this bracing coast.

This book is arranged in five chapters, and reflects the division of the county into three county council areas based on the historic divisions that emerged in the Middle Ages. After local government reorganisation in 1974, each of the three counties divided into two, with Lincoln as a city council. The far north was briefly merged with the East Riding of Yorkshire, but has regained its independence with the abolition of the spurious and much-hated county of Humberside. Chapter 1 tours the area of Lindsey in the north, while chapter 2 visits Lincoln and some villages round about the city. Chapter 3 tours the area of the county or 'parts' of Kesteven in the south-west, while chapter 4 follows an itinerary through the former area of the county or 'parts' of Holland. The last chapter tours the seaside resorts of the east coast in all their exuberantly cheerful splendour. The views of Skegness, however, capture a rather more sedate phase in its history. I hope you enjoy this selection of historic views and come to admire the county of Tennyson, Isaac Newton, John Wesley, William Wayneflete, Sir John Franklin, Matthew Flinders, Tony Jacklin, Ted Moult, Archbishop Whitgift and St Gilbert of Sempringham. If you are already a 'Yellow Belly', I need hardly sing the praises of Lincolnshire: you know its virtues already.

GAINSBOROUGH, SILVER STREET c1955 G145008

Each chapter can be followed as a self-contained tour. This first one starts on the banks of the River Trent and crosses the grain of the county: the limestone ridge, the chalk Wolds, the flat lands between the hills and the knobbly coastal sand dunes. Gainsborough, an ancient market town, was also a busy river port; here we look up Silver Street, which led from the river wharves and warehouses to the market place.

GAINSBOROUGH, MARKET PLACE c1955 G145009

Gainsborough was briefly England's capital in 1013, when the Danish king Sweyn Forkbeard, father of King Canute, ruled. He also died and was buried here in February 1014. Here we see the 1891 Town Hall with its tottering facade shored up. A year later, in 1956, it received its present insipid Neo-Georgian frontage.

GAINSBOROUGH, THE OLD HALL c1955 G145001

The Old Hall, very much the finest building in the town and now largely surrounded by Victorian housing, sits in its grassy square, a potent reminder of the town's great medieval past. The mansion of the mighty 15th-century De Burgh family, with a great central hall and long side wings, it is a miracle it survived, having at various times been a prison, a factory and tenements.

HEMSWELL, WELDON ROAD c1955 H316004

East of Gainsborough the Market Rasen road climbs the Lincoln Cliff, the limestone ridge which runs due north from Lincoln at about two hundred feet above sea level. In its lee is the old Roman road, Ermine Street, while at its foot, on the spring line, are a line of villages, mostly built from the local limestone. This one, Hemswell is well known for its maypole.

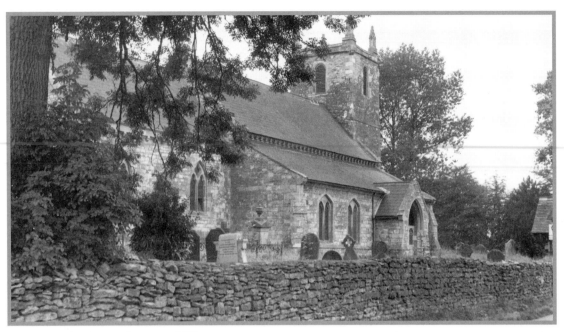

HEMSWELL, ALL SAINTS CHURCH c1955 H316006

Behind a dry stone wall All Saints Church sits in the centre of the winding main street of the village. Its tower dates from the 1760s; the bulk of the remainder was rebuilt in the 1860s, although there is medieval work inside, including the nave arcade.

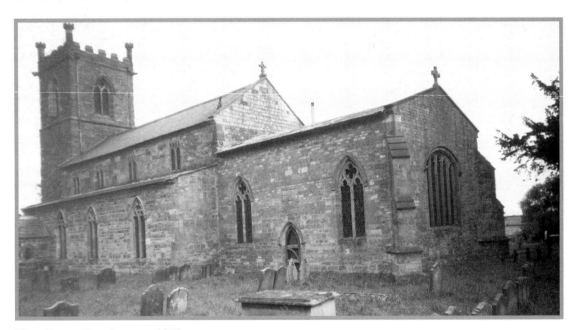

WEST RASEN, THE CHURCH c1955 W379002

Moving east off the Limestone Cliff, our route descends towards the clay vale that runs along the western edge of The Wolds. Apart from All Saints church, West Rasen is noted for its 15th-century pack horse bridge which crosses the River Rase, from which the Rasens are named, and which descends from The Wolds to merge with the Ancholme to head north to the River Humber.

MARKET RASEN, THE TOWN HALL CINEMA c1955 M231002
The town, separated from The Wolds to the east by thin sandy moors, now mostly afforested, became the main market for a wide area in the 16th century, and changed its name from East to Market Rasen. The Town Hall, in the 1950s a cinema, was demolished; now a gruesome 1960s Co-op mars the north-west corner of the Market Place, which has the fine parish church to its north side.

MARKET RASEN
Queen Street c1955 M231030
This view looks north towards the Market Place and captures well the
character of this market town, most of whose 19th- and late 18th-century
buildings still line the streets. Behind the tree on the right is the grand
stone front of the old Corn Exchange built in 1854, now solicitors' offices,
and on the left the fine hanging sign of The Gordon Arms pub.

MARKET RASEN, THE RACECOURSE c1955 M231035
East of the town, on the Louth Road, is Lincolnshire's only racecourse, since Lincoln's closed some years ago.
A National Hunt course, it opened in 1924, and the grandstand and buildings in this view, almost new in 1955,
remain virtually unaltered to this day; a further stand was added in 1967. Racing had taken place before 1924, of
course, on the sandy moors east of the town.

TEALBY, THE VILLAGE c1960 T216013
This chapter gives a snapshot of north Lincolnshire in the 1950s, as all the views were taken then: our tour takes
us next to Tealby, a pretty village at the western foot of The Wolds. All Saints church, higher up the village, has a
massive Norman tower, and the church is built in the local iron-rich brown limestone. Tealby is on the long-
distance waymarked footpath which runs from the Humber to Oakham via Lincoln.

TEALBY
Bayons Manor c1960

Bayons Manor was built by the uncle of Lincolnshire's famous son, Alfred Lord Tennyson. Uncle Charles was determined to underline the family's lineage and added the name 'D'Eyncourt' to Tennyson and built himself a medieval castle in the 1830s, vulgarly bedecked with coats of arms and heraldic badges. The mansion was demolished in 1965, but two lodges and other fragments remain.

LUDFORD MAGNA
The Post Office c1955

Ludford is a now a single-street village on the Louth to Gainsborough road at the head of the River Bain, which flows south through the Wolds to join the River Witham. Once Ludford Parva to the west and Ludford Magna to the east, the settlements are now merged. The post office cum garage is now a house named, unsurprisingly, The Old Post Office. To the left is the churchyard wall.

TEALBY, BAYONS MANOR c1960 T216005

LUDFORD MAGNA, THE POST OFFICE c1955 L509010

LUDFORD MAGNA, MAIN STREET c1955 L509003

This view looks east along the main street. The brick barn on the left at Red House Farm and the iron field fence remain, but the houses on the right have been altered and a few demolished, including the single-storey one on the corner of the quaintly-named Fanny Hands Lane.

BINBROOK, MARKET PLACE c1955 B536006

Binbrook, on the side of a valley of the rolling western part of The Wolds north of Ludford, was once a prosperous small market town with two parish churches. This view looks north across the sloping Market Place with the parish water pump on its island protected by bollards. Now improved and the island enlarged, the lamp is now a copy of a period one.

BINBROOK, THE SQUARE c1955 B536001

The north side of the Market Place has seen many recent changes: The Marquis of Granby, partly dating from 1695, was restored in 1999 and the paint removed from its stonework. Oscar Cook is now empty, while the roof has been lowered to the left part of the centre building. The hall up the hill on the left dates from 1914.

LOUTH, MERCER ROW c1955 L305035

Louth was a prosperous, compact market town serving a large area of the central Wolds. Its revival in the late 18th and early 19th centuries resulted in some fine town building and re-fronting of earlier buildings. Mercer Row is a good example, and the Georgian shop window to the right survives intact. The town is more famous, though, for its superb and grand church, crowned by its 295 feet high spire, built in the early 1500s at a cost of £305.

SALTFLEET, THE MILL c1955 S479012

Moving east off The Wolds, our tour reaches the flat land between them and the sea, with its high line of rolling marram-grassed sand dunes as a backdrop. Saltfleet lies just behind the dunes, but is a remnant of the medieval town and port a little further east, long washed away by the sea. The brick tower windmill of 1770 and 1890 survives, minus its sails, and has been well-converted into a house.

SALTFLEET, THE MANOR HOUSE c1955 S479011

North of the old windmill is the Manor House in mid seventeenth-century brick, which retains its original cross windows. It is said that Oliver Cromwell slept here after a Civil War skirmish at Winceby, so it would have to date from before the 1640s. The big tree has gone, and the outbuilding, whose steps can be seen at the left is now a single ruined wall.

TRUSTHORPE, THE POST OFFICE c1955 T217010

Almost swallowed up by the caravan sites to the east that merge Mablethorpe with Sutton on Sea, Trusthorpe clings to some independence. Trusthorpe Post Office is on the road to Thorpe, and is in a late Victorian projection from the left bay of a late 18th-century small farmhouse. The big tree remains, but the fence has gone and the mellow clay pantiles of the roof have been replaced.

TRUSTHORPE, ST PETER'S CHURCH c1955 T217025

The brick parish church is well away from the older surviving cottages and stands next to the Old Rectory, an early 19th-century small villa with a hipped roof. Of the medieval church, only the chancel arch survives; the tower dates from 1606, the nave from 1842 and the chancel was rebuilt in 1931. There is now a clock face above the belfry opening, otherwise the view is unchanged.

HUTTOFT, THE CHURCH c1960 H479301

HUTTOFT
The Church c1960

The village lies three miles inland along what passes for a ridge in this flat country between the Wolds and the sand dunes. The church is a curious mix of greenstone and limestone giving a patchwork quilt effect, while the chancel is in brick. The 13th-century tower windows below the belfry are studded with carved dogtooth mouldings. Beyond is the school of 1874, while the foreground is now occupied by bungalows.

ALFORD
The Church c1955

Alford is a most attractive small market town on the eastern edge of The Wolds, noted for its thatched Manor House in West Street, a 16th-century hall house with crosswings, all encased in brick in 1661. Its market was first chartered in 1283; in this view the Market Place is beyond the medieval parish church, here partly screened by the 1906 Church Hall.

ALFORD, THE CHURCH c1955 A209011

ALFORD, WEST STREET c1950 A209012

ALFORD
West Street c1950

Here the photographer looks along West Street away from the Market Place. In the foreground are cottages, some thatched, while in the distance are some more urban later houses of two and three full storeys. The thatched cottages of one or one and a half storeys with dormer windows are more villagey in character: there are remarkably few thatched houses in towns, but in Alford even the Manor House is thatched.

◆

ALFORD
The Mill c1955

At the east end of the town is Alford Mill, a six-storey, five-sail mill built in 1813 by Sam Oxley, an Alford millwright. It is owned by Lincolnshire County Council and has been restored to full working order. A few windmills feature in this collection: Lincolnshire once had over seven hundred of them.

ALFORD, THE MILL c1955 A209026

SPILSBY, MARKET SQUARE c1955 S391009
Spilsby got its market charter in 1302, a little later than Alford, and its centrepiece is the rectangular market place. In this view we look south-west towards the parish church with its fine green sandstone 15th-century tower. Its chief glory, however, is inside: the splendid medieval, Tudor and Jacobean tombs and effigies of the aristocratic Bertie and Willoughby families.

SPILSBY, THE FRANKLIN MONUMENT c1955 S391007
Dominating the Market Place is this dignified bronze statue, erected in 1861, of Sir John Franklin, the arctic explorer, born in Spilsby in 1786. His last expedition found the North-West Passage around the north of Canada, but Franklin and his crews died in 1847 when his ships, 'Erebus' and 'Terror', were trapped in the Arctic ice.

SPILSBY
Market Street c1955 S391004
How are the mighty fallen! The petrol station in the centre of the market place was the Town Hall with an open arcaded ground floor, the arches now glazed. It dates from 1764, and surely deserved a better fate. The subterranean public conveniences by the Ovaltine poster have now been replaced by a neat hipped roofed above-ground facility.

SPILSBY, HIGH STREET c1955 S391028

This view looks the other way from photograph S391046. The former Town Hall is on the left with The White Hart in the distance on the right, its 18th-century facade concealing a 17th-century building. At the right Smalls of Spilsby, a clothing shop, remains to this day.

SPILSBY, HIGH STREET c1955 S391046

The High Street runs parallel to Market Place and Market Street; it is terminated to the east by Aveland House, a dignified three-storey late Georgian town house. Most of the street is unchanged, apart from one house on the left which was replaced by a 1960s building, now Somerfields supermarket. The late 19th-century shopfronts fortunately survive.

HORNCASTLE, MARKET PLACE c1955 H319012

Horncastle is one of the county's most ancient towns. There are still remains of its Roman walling which enclosed about seven acres. It was granted a market charter in 1230 and is focused around its market place, seen here. The triangular Market Place is dominated by the Gothic-style memorial to Edward Stanhope, MP from 1874 to 1893; it is a parody of an Eleanor Cross and was erected in 1894.

HORNCASTLE, THE BULL RING c1955 H319020

An important medieval town, it declined until the early 19th century when the Horncastle Navigation Canal opened, giving access to Lincoln and Boston. In this view the thatched King's Head on the left and the Red Lion in the distance are 17th-century buildings amid the early 19th-century three-storey ones, which belong to that later phase of economic prosperity.

LINCOLN, BRAYFORD POOL 1890 25620
Lincoln, the county town of Lincolnshire, is situated where the limestone ridge is cut through by the River Witham.
Brayford Pool, a busy inland port that connected Lincoln both to the River Trent via the Roman Foss Dyke and to
the sea via the Witham, is much changed now; its warehouses are mostly replaced by offices and flats, although the
three on the left are the sole survivors.

LINCOLN, HIGH STREET 1923 74633

The ornate obelisk of 1763 commemorates a chapel that once stood on High Bridge. On the left is the celebrated timber-framed 16th-century range of shops and dwellings built on the west side of the bridge. The buildings beyond the obelisk have now made way for the prestigious modern Waterside shopping centre.

LINCOLN
The Cathedral and Stonebow 1890 25654
This splendidly atmospheric view along the High Street looks across towards the great medieval minster church which dominates the city and the countryside for miles around. The bridge crosses the canalised Witham, and in the distance is Stone Bow arch. The obelisk on the bridge and most of the buildings have since been replaced. The church tower belongs to the church of St Peter At Arches, demolished in 1933.

LINCOLN, HIGH STREET c1950 L49039

This view looks south down the High Street from near High Bridge. The 11th-century tower of St Mary le Wigford church peers out amid the later commercial architecture. Medieval Lincoln expanded from the Roman walled town southwards along the Roman Ermine Street, which here becomes the High Street. Lloyds TSB on the right, built in 1900, has since lost its cupola, and Marks and Spencer has been rebuilt.

LINCOLN, THE GLORY HOLE 1906 55112A

The High Bridge timber-framed buildings had got into a deplorable state by the 20th century, and were extensively restored and rebuilt in 1900 by William Watkins, who also added the three dormer windows. Here we look east along the River Witham, flowing out of Brayford Pool, with the High Street reached by steps from each bank. All other buildings have been rebuilt; those on the right are the modern Marks and Spencers.

LINCOLN, HIGH STREET 1923 74636

This view shows the ornate cast-iron balcony of the Saracen's Head Hotel, now shops, and the tower of St Peter at Arches beyond Stone Bow, built in 1720, demolished in 1933 and largely rebuilt in Lamb Gardens as St Giles Church at the instigation of the then vicar. The statues in the niches on Stone Bow are the Archangel Gabriel and the Virgin Mary.

LINCOLN, THE GUILDHALL 1890 25658

Through Stone Bow we look back across the setts to its rear, with the High Street stretching away into the distance through the archway. To the right is John Gibson's dignified Italianate bank of 1883, now the Nat West and well restored. It towers over Stone Bow and is one of the city's finest Victorian commercial buildings.

LINCOLN
Stone Bow 1901 46773

Lincoln's celebrated Stone Bow is the later 15th-century medieval gate into the walled town, above which is the basically Tudor city Guildhall. All was much restored by Pearson in the 1880s: he added the battlements, for example. The left-hand and centre archways are least altered. This view shows a bustling mid-morning Lincoln; the florid Flemish-style bank on the left dating from the 1890s survives from this prosperous era.

Lincoln, High Street c1950 L49028

Lincoln, Steep Hill 1906 55115

Lincoln
High Street c1950

We are now within the Roman and medieval city walls. The view north along High Street is terminated by a white gabled building, now O'Neills pub. The road deviates to the right here, to tackle the climb of 150 feet up The Strait and Steep Hill. This view shows some of the pre-war commercial rebuilding, including an Art Deco Burton's on the left and a Neo-Georgian Boots.

◆

Lincoln
Steep Hill 1906

Beyond The Strait, Steep Hill commences with The Jew's House, a Norman stone house of the 1170s, before climbing more steeply up towards the cathedral and castle on the top of the hill. The narrow, precipitous street is pedestrianised and thronged with toiling tourists in summer. Mr Haigh's Toy and Fancy Repository on the left is now a gift and games shop: a kind of continuity.

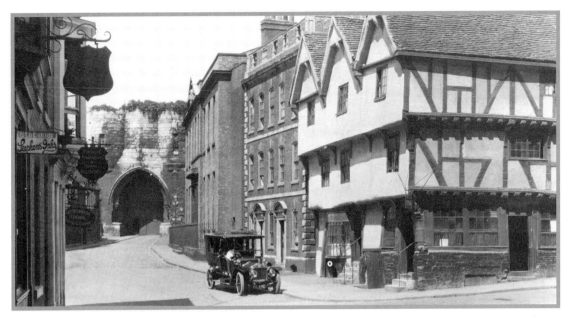

LINCOLN, CASTLE HILL 1906 55115A

Reaching the top of Steep Hill, the photographer looks west from Exchequer Gate, the medieval gatehouse into the cathedral close, towards the Castle gatehouse. The three-gabled and jettied timber-framed building of 1543 on the right was restored in 1929 and is now a tourist information centre. It contrasts with the fine Georgian sash-windowed building beyond.

LINCOLN, THE CASTLE GATES c1955 L49106

Inside the Castle, the photographer looks back to the gatehouse, which is basically 14th-century over a Norman archway, although the drum towers on this side are early 19th-century. The Norman castle building involved demolishing over 160 Anglo-Saxon houses; since the Middle Ages it has served as a prison and assize courts. This concludes our brief tour of Lincoln itself.

DODDINGTON, THE VILLAGE 1906 55116

Our brief tour of Lincoln's surrounding villages begins to the west in Doddington village. Although only five miles to the west, it has avoided the expansion of villages such as Skellingthorpe or North Hykeham. It is still a small estate village at the gates of Doddington Hall, a large late Elizabethan mansion built for Thomas Taylor, Recorder to the bishop of Lincoln, and often open to the public.

DODDINGTON, THE CHURCH 1906 55117

The stone walls of St Peter's Church, to the north of the forecourt to Doddington Hall, are a marked contrast to the mellow red brick of the Hall, which might be by Robert Smythson, the architect of Hardwick Hall. Mostly rebuilt by Thomas Lumby in the 1770s in a fairly correct Gothic, the church has a more cheery Strawberry Hill Gothick west tower and spire.

NAVENBY, HIGH STREET c1965 N132007

South of Lincoln a string of villages grew up along the western edge of the limestone ridge, mostly along the spring line. Navenby is a small market town with wide, airy views over the Trent valley to the west. There is a fine church, noted for its Decorated Gothic chancel, and a broad main street, once the market place. Beyond the telephone box, still here, the shop was rebuilt recently, but otherwise there has been little change.

METHERINGHAM, HIGH STREET c1955 M232011

Roughly east of Navenby, where the limestone descends to the flat east of the county, Metheringham is a large village with a mix of stone and brick older houses interspersed with Victorian and later development. In this view the Beehive shop and the dormered cottage beyond survive, but the buildings beyond have been rebuilt for Townsends and the Post Office.

WADDINGTON, HIGH STREET c1960 W2006

BRANSTON, THE CHURCH c1955 B512001

WADDINGTON
High Street c1960
To the east of Waddington is a vast Royal Air Force station, but the old village core with its mellow limestone houses and cottages remains remarkably unspoilt. The medieval church was destroyed by bombs in World War II intended for Lincoln or the RAF base, but in this view we look north past the Horse and Jockey pub in a view little changed since 1960.

◆

BRANSTON
The Church c1955
Branston, around its church, has delightful winding lanes; by the church stands Hainton House of 1765, a Georgian house of some dignity. All Saints Church is an interesting one, with Anglo-Saxon 'long and short work' quoins to the nave and an Anglo-Saxon tower with an elaborate Norman west doorway and arcading. The spire is 15th-century.

WRAGBY, MARKET PLACE c1965 W382010

East of Lincoln, Wragby is a market town on the Horncastle and Skegness road which is very busy at weekends and in summer. It received a market charter from Charles II, and at its centre is a big triangular Market Place. The garage has now been replaced by public toilets. In the distance are the Almshouses, founded by Sir Edmund Turnor in the 17th century but rebuilt in 1840.

WRAGBY, THE CHURCH c1965 W382001

The parish church lies east of the Almshouses, which can be seen beyond the chancel. Built in yellow brick in 1839 in what is known as 'Commissioners Gothic', the present All Saints was relocated by Sir Edmund Turnor to this site, a quarter of a mile away from the site of the medieval church, the chancel of which only disappeared in 1980.

GRANTHAM, MARKET PLACE 1893 33256

Chapter Three is a tour of the rolling oolitic limestone south-west part of Lincolnshire, until 1974 the County of Kesteven. We start in the Market Place of Grantham, a town of 30,000 whose medieval wealth was based on wool from the sheep grazing the Kesteven fields. Later an industrial town, it retains much of its Georgian and Victorian brick rebuilding of what had been a stone town.

GRANTHAM, MARKET PLACE c1955 G43034

The obelisk seen in photograph No 33256 had been replaced by the Market Cross before the 1950s, and Broughton's shop was rebuilt in 1904; it is now the Trattoria Sorrento. Behind the photographer is the 1597 water conduit, while in the distance is the stone front of the Angel Hotel. Hill's, now G & M's restaurant, has since lost its semi-circular window and parapet for a gable.

GRANTHAM
The Angel Hotel 1893

The Angel Hotel is a remarkable late 15th-century stone-built inn, rebuilt on the site of a Knights Templar hostel where King John had held court in 1213; in this building Richard III signed the Duke of Buckingham's death warrant. The central archway with its oriel window above led into the inn yard, where there is a long brick range dated 1776.

◆

GRANTHAM
The Angel Hotel 1904

The Angel's sash windows replace the original windows, although the medieval stone hood moulds survive, as do the buttresses. The building to the right in photograph 33258 has, by 1904, been replaced by the elaborate buff terra cotta Flemish-style Boots building. The buildings beyond have been somewhat mutilated now, and one has been replaced by a taller Neo-Georgian bank, now the Yorkshire Bank.

GRANTHAM, THE ANGEL HOTEL 1893 33258

GRANTHAM, THE ANGEL HOTEL 1904 51638

GRANTHAM, HIGH STREET c1955 G43024

As we look south down High Street we can see that many of the buildings survive today, including the dormered building on the far left. Bearing in mind that this was the Great North Road , the A1, which now by-passes the town, the scene is remarkably tranquil. Nowadays Grantham is most well-known as the birthplace of Margaret Thatcher; her father's shop in North Parade had a brief apotheosis as The Premier Restaurant.

GRANTHAM, HIGH STREET 1904 51628

Sad to say, this is an archive view, for since 1904 all the dignified Georgian and early Victorian buildings on the right have been replaced as far as the middle distance building with a corniced parapet. More survives on the left; in the distance are the pilasters of Newton and Derry's building to give the viewer a point of reference.

GRANTHAM, HIGH STREET C-----*1955 G43022

The George Hotel on the left, a very large coaching inn on the old Great North Road built in 1780, has now been successfully converted into The George Shopping Centre. Beyond it, where the road narrows, is a good building of the 1840s with paired giant pilasters, now Newton and Derry, estate agents. On the right-hand side of the road there has been much rebuilding of varying quality.

GRANTHAM, ST PETER'S HILL 1904 51632

At the south end of the High Street the road widens to a pleasant green, formerly a market place. At its south end is an 1891 statue of Frederick Tollemache, the town's MP for nearly 50 years from 1826. To the right is the town hall of 1867, now the Guildhall Centre, while the house to its right was replaced by a library and museum in the 1950s. To its right buildings of 1884 are now The Tollemache Inn.

GRANTHAM, WESTGATE 1904 51631

To the west the Melton Mowbray road reaches the town centre via Westgate, a wide street seen here looking north-east towards Market Place. Most of the buildings in this view survive, and even the painted lettering on Atlas House can be seen through later paint. In the distance is the 14th-century spire of Grantham's superb parish church, St Wulfram.

GRANTHAM, THE BEE HIVE INN 1893 33262

Back to the east of St Peter's Hill, the photographer looks north along Castlegate, with the Beehive Inn on the left; the leaves hide a beehive set in the tree, which is still there. The name sign 'East Street' has been reused on a 1960s replacement for the buildings on the right, while beyond the Gothic-style school soars the 280 feet tower and spire of St Wulfram's.

GRANTHAM, THE GRAMMAR SCHOOL 1890 27850
Facing the churchyard on the north side of Church Street is the oldest building in the King's School, built just before 1528 as a chantry school. This range is now the library and was, as a plaque informs us, where Isaac Newton was a pupil in the 1650s. No 1 on the right, a good 18th-century stone front, is now a Centre for Industrial Studies.

GRANTHAM, AVENUE ROAD 1904 51630
East from St Peter's Hill, Avenue Road descends towards the River Witham, lined by middle-class late Victorian semi-detached villas. There are now fewer trees, and several of the houses are offices or hotels. At the left is the rock-faced stone St Peter's Hill United Reformed Church of 1869. Many of the villas beyond are of round about that date.

GRANTHAM, THE BARRACKS 1893 33267

GRANTHAM
The Barracks 1893
Across the Witham, Avenue Road becomes Beacon Lane and passes the old barracks of 1858 and 1872 of the Royal South Lincolnshire Militia, now occupied by an auctioneers and valuers. It is a craggy, rock-faced stone castle with a large courtyard. In this view the militia can be seen drilling in the field beyond, now a sports ground.

◆

SKILLINGTON
The Village c1965
Moving south from Grantham, out into the oolitic limestone country towards the Leicestershire border, we reach Skillington; it has a good range of stone houses, and a parish church with some Anglo-Saxon work in the nave and an attractive 14th-century broach spire. Far House and Tylers Farm to the left are 17th-century, while 19th-century houses are on the right.

SKILLINGTON, THE VILLAGE c1965 S482011

COLSTERWORTH, THE VILLAGE c1960 C428010

This view on the Stainby Road, with the houses on the left fronting onto the High Street, which runs left from the signpost, hardly does justice to this large and attractive village in whose part-Norman parish church the great Isaac Newton was baptised. He was born in Woolsthorpe Manor, an early 17th-century house, in 1643; Woolsthorpe is a hamlet immediately north-west of the village.

WOOLSTHORPE, THE VILLAGE c1955 W363020

This is not Isaac Newton's Woolsthorpe, but the village west of Grantham in rolling countryside right on the Leicestershire border; it has fine views of Belvoir Castle a mile away on its hill on the other side of the valley of the River Devon. Further up the road is the Victorian parish church, which replaced one of 1791 which itself replaced the medieval one, apparently burned down in the Civil War.

HARLAXTON HOUSE 1890 22864

Nearer Grantham, this gigantic Elizabethan palace is in fact 19th-century. Gregory Gregory, a bachelor, was probably responsible for as much of the design as his architects, Anthony Salvin and later William Burn, as it rose slowly throughout the 1830s and 1840s. This view is from the mile-long north-west drive: the visitor approaches a spectacularly busy mansion encrusted in turrets, bay windows, elaborate chimneys, cupolas and much more. Harlaxton Manor is now owned by the American University of Evansville.

HARLAXTON, THE SCHOOLS 1890 22866

In the village itself, Gregory Gregory's hand is everywhere, as befits an estate village nestling at the gates of a great country house in its park. This is the school (now houses) which Gregory provided and embellished: more Tudor than the Tudors. Beneath all this timber-framing, turrets and fancy brick chimneys is an 18th-century cottage. Beyond is the crocketted spire of the church, which also received the Gregory Treatment: it is very much over-restored.

BELTON, BELTON HOUSE 1904 51644

North of Grantham, set in its seven hundred acre landscaped deer park, Belton House was begun in 1685; it is architecturally conservative for that date with its cupola and balustraded flat roof. It was built by Sir John Brownlow, using Lincolnshire's own superlative building stone, the Ancaster limestone, and was acquired from the seventh Lord Brownlow by the National Trust in 1984.

GRANTHAM, BELTON HOUSE c1960 G43074

This view of the north or garden front shows the design of this beautiful and well-proportioned house with its projecting side wings and pedimented centre, the whole forming a letter H plan. The cupola and balustrades were removed by James Wyatt in the 1770s but, happily, were reinstated after 1867.

GRANTHAM, BELTON HOUSE, ORANGERY RESTAURANT c1960 G43087

Well before the National Trust took over, Belton was often open to the public. The Orangery was converted into a restaurant and tea room, a good use for the fine airy building designed by Jeffry Wyatville and built in 1820. Wyatville was really a Wyatt, the nephew of James Wyatt, gaining the smarter French-sounding name with George III's permission while working on Windsor Castle.

SLEAFORD, THE MONUMENT c1950 S483029

Sleaford has fragments of a castle, built by Alexander, the princely Bishop of Lincoln, in the 1120s, but its function as a market town for north Kesteven is undimmed. This view looks north along South Gate past the extraordinarily grandiose statue in its towering medieval-style spired canopy to a 19th-century MP, Henry Handley, which dates from 1850.

SLEAFORD, SOUTHGATE c1950 S483030

Moving north, just beyond the Handley Memorial, and heading for the Market Place, we see buildings mostly from the late 18th- and 19th-century phase of Sleaford's prosperity, with the castellated house on the corner of Handley Street, dated 1907, as its last gasp. To the south of the railway are the former Maltings, built in the 1890s on a colossal scale, and an industrial monument to one of Sleaford's major industries.

SLEAFORD, NORTHGATE c1950 S483032

At the end of South Gate is the Market Place, which has on its east side one of Lincolnshire's finest churches. Here, where South Gate meets North Gate, are the town's finest commercial buildings, such as the HSBC bank of 1903 on the left and the Sessions House of 1830 in Gothick style with a pointed arched ground arcade.

SLEAFORD, WEST BANKS c1955 S483038

Sleaford is built on the banks of the River Slea which splits into two branches no more than streams in size. This view looks east along West Banks, with its numerous small bridges, to the mainly late Victorian artisan cottages (some are dated 1901). To the south are further artisan terraces and short side streets. The early 19th-century cottages on the left were lost in the 1960s.

HECKINGTON, HIGH STREET c1955 H63003

Five miles east of Sleaford, Heckington is a village widely known for its superb 14th-century Decorated Gothic parish church with its 185 foot high spire, rich carvings and sinuous window tracery. Here we look along the High Street, where most of the houses and cottages survive on the left but only No 62, then an antique shop, on the right. The village is also known for its windmill which has no less than eight sails.

EDENHAM, THE VILLAGE C1955 B511013

Heading south towards Bourne, the route diverts north-east of the town to Edenham, a delightful village on the east bank of the winding East Glen River, whose church has many remarkable monuments to the Bertie family of nearby Grimsthorpe Castle. The village has mostly limestone buildings; the cedars remain in its churchyard, which is dominated by the pinnacle-topped 15th-century tower. The cottage on the right has been replaced by a stone bungalow further back from the roadside.

BOURNE, NORTH STREET 1952 B511003

Bourne, at the junction where two Roman roads met, had a Roman station to guard the Car Dyke, the great Roman dyke 56 miles long and still surviving for long stretches. Later, Bourne became a market town with a (now largely vanished) castle and a Norman priory founded in 1138, now the parish church. Here we look from a bustling market place with the stalls spreading into North Street; the three gables of The Angel Hotel are on the left.

BOURNE, MARKET SQUARE C1955 B511002

The Market Square is at the busy cross-roads in the centre of this delightful small town. The Gothic-style drinking fountain of 1860 has been relocated to the cemetery in South Road, presumably to save it from the traffic, while the good stone-tile-roofed building beyond on the corner of South Street is still Harrison and Dunn's shop today.

STAMFORD, FROM THE WATER MEADOWS 1922 72296

Stamford, one of England's most attractive and historic towns, is only just in Lincolnshire. The River Welland is the boundary between it and Northamptonshire. This view from the water meadows is a very well known one and relatively little changed, although it would look very different to a late medieval traveller when there were fourteen parish church towers in this view.

STAMFORD, THE TOWN BRIDGE 1922 72314
Another view along the Welland towards Town Bridge, over which the old Great North Road crossed into Lincolnshire. Built in 1849, it replaced four arches of a medieval one, while to the right is Lord Burghley's Hospital, built in 1597 on the site of an older hospital founded in the 1170s. A Norman culvert and masonry survive from this earlier building. Opposite is the mansard-roofed Anchor Inn.

STAMFORD, THE GEORGE HOTEL 1922 72305
Much of 18th-century Stamford's trade came from its location on the Great North Road, and it had numerous coaching inns. The George is probably the best known, an inn since 1568 and noted for its sign spanning the road. Beyond is part of Lord Burghley's Hospital, then the river, and up the hill in Stamford proper the elegant 160 foot tower and spire of St Mary's church, a superb 13th-century Early English Gothic structure.

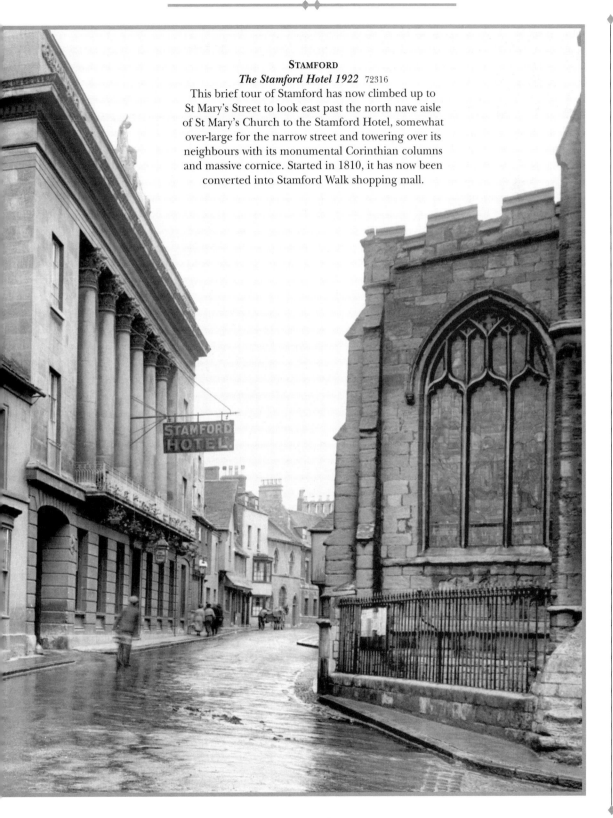

STAMFORD
The Stamford Hotel 1922 72316
This brief tour of Stamford has now climbed up to St Mary's Street to look east past the north nave aisle of St Mary's Church to the Stamford Hotel, somewhat over-large for the narrow street and towering over its neighbours with its monumental Corinthian columns and massive cornice. Started in 1810, it has now been converted into Stamford Walk shopping mall.

STAMFORD, ST MARY'S STREET 1922 72309

As we move further west, we see a part of St Mary's Street with an interesting mix of buildings with alleys leading down to the river front and The Meadows. The gabled building is flanked by two of these alleys, Bugle Lane to its right and Olde Barn Passage to its left. Now Paul Richman, a clothes shop, the first floor window has been restored and the render removed from the stonework, setting off the 1656 date-stone.

STAMFORD
Brookes Court 1922

This view looks up Olde Barn Passage past Brookes Court. In the distance is Richman's and St Mary's Street. Barton's, a 17th-century timber-framed building with a Collyweston stone tile roof, is now L'Incontro restaurant. This view captures the character of Stamford's numerous alleys and steep narrow lanes off the main streets.

STAMFORD
Red Lion Square 1922

This view looks north towards All Saints Church, whose massive tower and elegant crocketted spire dominate its battlemented nave, chancel and aisles. To its right Barn Hill climbs gently north-west, a street of almost unspoilt Georgian houses.

STAMFORD, BROOKES COURT 1922 72313

STAMFORD, RED LION SQUARE 1922 72299

STAMFORD
Market Place 1922 72298
North from St Mary's Street, St John's Street leads past St John's Church into Red Lion Square,
the market place. In this view, the photographer looks south-east back past the corner of High
Street to St John's Street and St John's 15th-century west tower. To the left is St Mary's Church
spire. The HSBC bank with its five Dutch gables is of 1848, and somewhat over-dominant.

STAMFORD
High Street 1922 72302
Our photographer now proceeds east along the High Street, a relatively narrow street with a mix of 17th-century and later fronts, now pedestrianised. The gabled Grant's butcher's shop has been removed to the Kirkgate Museum in York, Singer's has lost its elegant shopfronts and has been texture-coated, and Star Stores opposite was rebuilt in rough replica in 1982 for The Halifax.

STAMFORD, HIGH STREET 1922 72301

Further east, at the junction with Ironmonger Street, the quality of the Georgian stone or stucco façades on the right is evident, while on the left or south side there is more variety. No 55, beyond the gabled front, has a fine Georgian stone façade to a 16th-century timber-framed building. The railings to the left, now gone, bounded the churchyard of St Michael's Church of 1836, bizarrely converted into a shopping mall in 1982.

STAMFORD, IRONMONGER STREET 1922 72312

As we look south down Ironmonger Street, the view is terminated by St Michael's Church, now gruesomely converted into shops, but I suppose in some way 'saved' from physical if not spiritual destruction. No 13, on the far right, now a hairdresser, has a facia covering the lunette window, but the rest of the shopfront remains to ornament this fine and quite architecturally varied side street.

MARKET DEEPING
The Market Place 1900 M116301
Chapter Four takes a tour from east of
Stamford into the fenland of
Lincolnshire, mostly in the former
administrative county of Holland, very
much the flat country. As its name
implies, Market Deeping is a market
town with a large, triangular market
place, lined with pubs such as The Bull
for the farmers and coaching inns for
travellers, including The Deeping Stage
on the left and The King's Head Inn
on the right.

MARKET DEEPING
The Market Place c1955

Half a century after photograph M116301, the Market place is much tidier, with kerbs, grass and flower beds, and it has parked cars in the centre. These occupy the site of houses demolished in 1848 that had been built as encroachments along the centre of the Market Place. The gable on the left belongs to the old Town Hall, a Gothic-style building of 1835. Behind the frontages beyond is The Precincts, a new shopping mall.

◆

MARKET DEEPING
Church Street c1955

Church Street is much quieter, away from the A16 Stamford to Spalding road. Another wide street, and also laid out as a market, it has many good stone houses, including almshouses of 1877 on the left and several pubs. The view along the grass-verged straight street is closed by the dignified 15th-century tower of St Guthlac's church.

MARKET DEEPING, THE MARKET PLACE C1955 M116040

MARKET DEEPING, CHURCH STREET C1955 M116007

DEEPING ST JAMES, THE CROSS c1965 D150005

East of Market Deeping and joined to it is Deeping St James village. At its heart is this curious structure in medieval stone. The former village cross, it was built in the 15th century, but in 1819 the cross shaft was removed and the base, quite extraordinarily, was converted into the village lock-up.

DEEPING ST JAMES, THE CHURCH AND THE CROSS c1965 D150001

Looking north-west past the village cross, we see the church with its curiously plain tower and mean spire. Closer examination reveals that the tower was in fact built in 1717 in a version of Gothic that fails to convince. Inside, by contrast, the late 12th-century nave arcades are serene and perfectly proportioned, as befits a church owned by the mighty Thorney Abbey.

DEEPING ST JAMES, CHURCH STREET c1965 D150004

The village itself is a mix of stone and local brick, as in the terrace on the right. Kingscote on the far left is dated 1892, while the two gables in the middle distance, with the shop, belong to a U-plan house with a date stone '1688', but much altered.

CROWLAND, THE BRIDGE 1894 34833

The town grew up at the gates of the abbey on a low island amid the surrounding marshes, receiving its charter in 1142. Apart from the Abbey, the town is famous for the 14th-century triangular bridge, seen here from West Street. The streets now no longer have streams flowing down them, so the bridge is a redundant curiosity in a town with many good things architecturally.

CROWLAND, THE ABBEY 1894 34831
The abbey, in the Middle Ages the richest in Lincolnshire, was built on the site of the 7th-century St Guthlac's timber hermitage. It is now a fragment: the nave north aisle is now the parish church with a monumental 15th-century tower capped by a squat spire. The remains of the rest of the abbey church are a tantalising glimpse of an opulent past, while all the monastic buildings have vanished.

SPALDING, MARKET PLACE c1960 S388218

Reaching Spalding we are in the heart of the bulb-growing country; the surrounding countryside is a glorious carpet of daffodils, tulips and other flowers at different times of the year. This view looks towards the Jacobean-style Town Hall. Its bell turret was replaced in 1974 by the South Holland Centre, an extremely busy building architecturally but quite enjoyable.

SPALDING, MARKET PLACE c1955 S388171

This view looks west on market day. The White Hart Hotel's stuccoed front dates from about 1714. It is currently (March 2000) closed . The Natwest bank to its right is over-scaled 1930s Neo-Georgian, while to the left of the White Hart two buildings have recently also been replaced in pallid Neo-Georgian.

SPALDING, HIGH BRIDGE c1960 S388227

Spalding's townscape is 'made' by the River Welland, which bisects the town. There are roads along each bank and houses face the river, giving it a slightly Dutch feel. Indeed, there are some fine Georgian houses, particularly on the east side near the good parish church. Here we look towards High Bridge of 1838. Berrills and the buildings beyond have been demolished to make way for road improvements and a riverside walk.

LONG SUTTON, MARKET PLACE c1950 L484011

Moving east along B-roads zig-zagging through the Fens, we reach Long Sutton. This market town is noted for its rare 13th-century lead spire and late Norman nave. In the Market Place at first sight all looks broadly unchanged, but since 1950 The Bull has been entirely rebuilt in rough replica, and the Crown and Woolpack has had its stucco removed, but the chemist's shop is still a chemist, albeit no longer run by Norman Hounslow.

HOLBEACH, HIGH STREET c1955 H318016

West of Long Sutton and east of Spalding, Holbeach is another of Lincolnshire's numerous small market towns. It received its first market charter in 1252. The north side of High Street, on the right, has some dignified late 18th- and early 19th-century three-storey houses, including The Bell and The Chequers Hotels. On the left is the churchyard, and beyond is an Italianate building of the 1890s that plays a major townscape role.

HOLBEACH, HIGH STREET c1955 H318015

Further east, Franklins Outfitters, a mid 19th-century Italianate building on the right has gone, as have those in the distance on the left, to be replaced by the tepid Neo-Georgian Talbot Court. The 180 foot spire of All Saints can be seen beyond, but the most remarkable feature of the church is the north porch: this seems to be a re-used castle gatehouse, perhaps from Moulton Castle, five miles to the west.

HOLBEACH, HIGH STREET c1955 H318032

The photographer is now positioned east of Franklin's Outfitters, since demolished. The tall cluster of stacks to its right belongs to No 45, The Mansion House, a Georgian house set back from the street front, in which Sir Norman Angell was born, the winner of the 1933 Nobel Peace Prize.

DONINGTON, HIGH STREET c1965 D220020

Heading towards Boston, we reach Donington on the Grantham to Boston road, an attractive market town, once the centre of a flax and hemp trade with three hemp fairs a year. This view looks east from the Market Place along the High Street, not the most distinguished in Lincolnshire; however, the Red Cow is a coaching inn with an 18th-century refront to a 17th-century inn and has a former assembly room to its right.

DONINGTON, MARKET PLACE C1955 D220012

This view looks west from the Market Place into Station Street. Beyond the Black Bull inn sign are the three gables of No 2, Pointz House, in which captain Matthew Flinders, the explorer of Australian shores and seas, was born in 1774. The Black Bull itself is a 17th-century building refronted in the 18th century.

DONINGTON, HIGH STREET C1955 D220005

Further east, 18th-century Mansfield House on the right with its two canted bay windows and pedimented doorcase is the best building, while the one with three dormers beyond is now a county branch library. Behind the Hovis sign, a fire station has since been built, but the rendered building in the middle distance, The Black Swan, is still a pub today.

BOSTON, MARKET PLACE 1899 43296

Boston, Botolph's Town, was laid out along the banks of the River Witham some time around 1100, within the parish of nearby Skirbeck, and rapidly became a great port, although it only received its first charter in 1205 from King John. It acquired town walls in 1285, and in 1353 it wrested away Lincoln's wool staple. It was the wool trade that built the town, with its seething market and vast numbers of ships.

BOSTON
Market Place 1899 43295

The town centre is dominated by its very large triangular market place, which in its turn is visually overwhelmed by the mighty church steeple, completed in 1460 and universally known as the Boston Stump. Crowned by an octagonal lantern, it soars 272 feet above the town and can be seen from miles around, even from Lincoln. It served as a landmark for shipping, for the lantern used to have a beacon lit at night.

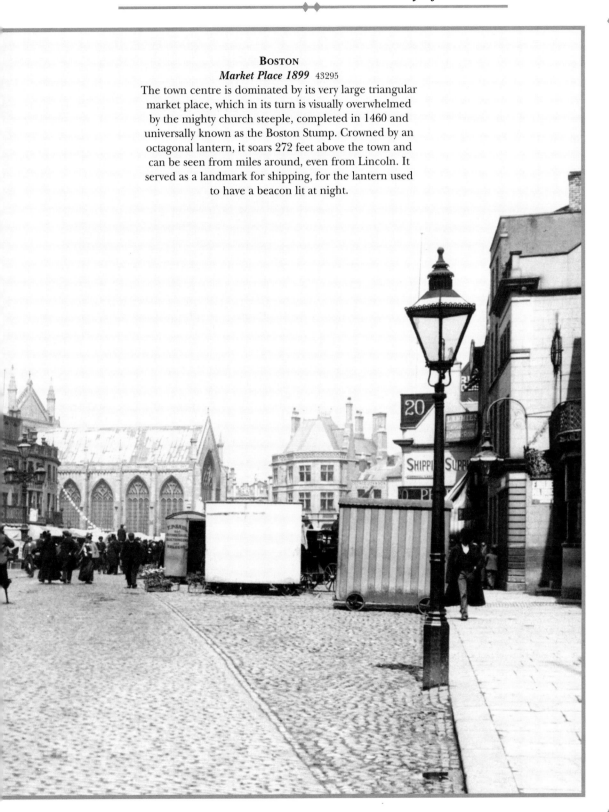

BOSTON, MARKET SQUARE C1955 B155044

Fifty years after photograph 43295, the buildings are mostly intact, as now. On the left is the Guildhall with its 18th-century façade, then the Rum Puncheon, now Martha's Pub. Benefit, in earlier views The Angel Hotel, is now an Edinburgh Woollen Mill shop. All the buildings between The Rum Puncheon and the church are in fact market encroachments, so the market place was once even larger.

BOSTON, SHODFRIARS HALL 1889 22274

In South Street, Shodfriars Hall is an echo of the four friaries established in the medieval town. In fact it was probably the hall of a trade guild, but in its present form it owes more to John Oldrid Scott's 'restoration' in 1874 than the Middle Ages. It probably had an open ground storey for trade, rather like Thaxted's Guildhall in Essex, but it is a splendid reminder of the town's medieval past.

BOSTON, HIGH STREET 1899 43300

The High Street, across the Witham via Town Bridge rebuilt in 1913, presents a mainly late Georgian character with mostly three-storey frontages to the pavement edge, but many of these conceal earlier buildings of medieval, Tudor and Stuart Boston. Several of those shown here have been demolished and rebuilt, including Wilson's on the right, but the oriel window in the middle distance on No 18 survives.

BOSTON, DOUGHTY QUAY 1890 26066

Further south, High Street opens up to the river, the buildings terminating in an elegant early 19th-century five-storey warehouse with a hipped roof: more like a very tall villa than a warehouse. The warehouses of Boston have suffered in recent years; the ones on the right on the opposite bank have been converted into flats, but the distant one has been, like so many of its companions, demolished.

BOSTON, TOWER STREET 1893 32065

BOSTON
Tower Street 1893
Tower Street, its houses mostly mid-Victorian terraces and semi-detached villas, some dated 1879 and 1880, has its vista closed by one of England's most stunningly effective buildings: the Boston Stump. It is actually across the river, but this view shows the tower's wonderful proportions and classical elegance superbly.

BOSTON
The Windmill c1965
Battle your way across or round the inner relief road that did so much damage to the town's historic fabric and cross the Maud Foster Drain into Willoughby Road, where Boston's celebrated Maud Foster Mill dominated the town's eastern growth beyond the town walls. Built in 1819, this five sailer, in working order, now has tea rooms in the mill warehouse whose weatherboarded bag hoist turret is visible between now-demolished houses.

BOSTON, THE WINDMILL c1965 B155096

BOSTON, THE DOCKS 1893 32078

Built south of the town, the new docks were 825 feet long by 450 feet wide and are still busy. However, none of the buildings survive, although the dock walls and the entrance abutments in the distance remain. Beyond is the medieval tower of Skirbeck church, the centre of the village in whose parish medieval Boston was planted: indeed the mighty St Botolph's church was a mere chapel of ease to Skirbeck until the 14th century.

BOSTON, THE DOCKS 1890 26082

Boston's Tudor decline was steep: the wool trade upon which the town had waxed fat faded away, and the river silted up. It was not until the 18th century that the town recovered, and the railway arrived in 1848. A new dock was authorised by Act of Parliament in 1881 and was opened in 1882, partly paid for by the Great Northern Railway, who extended a branch line to it.

BOSTON, HUSSEY TOWER 1893 32077

This mid 15th-century brick tower, here seen in rural tranquillity with cattle grazing, now sits amid football pitches near Boston College's Rochford Campus. The Boston Stump can be seen on the right. Built for the Hussey family, the tower came into the council's hands in 1544 after Lord Hussey was executed by Henry VIII. Built like a castle keep, it was attached to a long-vanished hall, and is clearly influenced by Tattershall Castle not far away.

CONINGSBY, THE MILL c1955 C429003

Heading north-west roughly parallel to the River Witham, we reach two small towns on either side of the River Bain, which meets the Witham a mile away at Dogdyke. Coningsby, on the south bank, has lost much of its historic character: in this view of Silver Street the house in front of the mill survives, but not the mill; all to the left has gone, and the road at the right has become a footpath.

CONINGSBY, SILVER STREET c1955 C429015

Tattershall and Coningsby lie just south of the last slopes of the Wolds, with the flat Fens stretching away to the south. This view looks to the north end of Silver Street and its junction with the High Street, the main Sleaford to Skegness Road. All on the left has gone; to the left, out of picture, is the parish church, whose tower has a giant clock face painted in its east elevation.

TATTERSHALL, THE CASTLE c1955 T15025

Across the Bain, Tattershall is altogether less ravaged by 1960s and later rebuilding. Due to the lack of building stone in this part of the county, brick made an early appearance; several major medieval brick buildings survive. We have already seen the Hussey Tower in Boston, while Lord Cromwell's mighty brick tower keep of the 1430s can be seen for miles across the flat Fens of Holland.

TATTERSHALL
THE GREEN c1955 T15021

The roughly rectangular Market Place (or village green) with its medieval cross is
surrounded by attractive houses with shops on the east side. To the south, across the
Sleaford to Skegness Road, an alley leads to Lord Cromwell's College just beyond
the road frontage buildings; it is another 15th-century brick building, known as the
Old College to distinguish it from the excavated remains of that near the church.

WAINFLEET ALL SAINTS, MARKET PLACE c1955 W550002

The town was probably established as a port on the Wainfleet Haven by Bardney Abbey, but by the 15th century the haven silted up and the port declined. The Haven became a continuation of the Steeping River, and the sea is now three miles away. At its centre is the square Market Place with a medieval market cross whose shaft can be seen to the left.

WAINFLEET ALL SAINTS, MAIN ROAD c1955 W550003

In this view we look back towards the Market Place along High Street with the Angel and the Red Lion in the middle distance on the left. Further south and out of picture, nearer the railway line, is Bateman's Brewery with its mainly 19th-century buildings. Founded in 1874 and still independent, Batemans slogan is well known: 'Good Honest Ales'.

WAINFLEET ALL SAINTS, HIGH STREET c1955 W550007

Back in the Market Place, the photographer looks south down the High Street. Cook's on the corner is still a newsagent and stationer, Goodnews. On the right are the two best pubs architecturally in the town, the Red Lion and the Angel Inn.

WAINFLEET ALL SAINTS, THE WOOLPACK HOTEL c1955 W550006

North from the Market Place, the High Street curves away past The Woolpack, now rendered and roughcast. Wainfleet is famous as the birthplace of William of Wayneflete, later Bishop of Winchester and founder of Winchester College school and Magdalen College, Oxford. Just off Market Place is the Wainfleet School of 1484, now the public library, another of Lincolnshire's medieval brick buildings, a long first floor hall with giant polygonal towers flanking the west front.

WAINFLEET ALL SAINTS, MARKET PLACE c1955 W550001
Back in the Market Place, the clock tower is an architecturally undistinguished brick structure with a stone plaque telling us that its foundation stone was laid on 26 January 1899. Beyond the late Victorian pair, The Manse and The Villa (with the timbered gable) tower over the pair of small cottages beside them.

BURGH LE MARSH, THE WINDMILL c1955 B513020
North of Wainfleet, on the Skegness to Lincoln road, Burgh le Marsh is a market town whose charter was granted in 1401. At its east end is another of Lincolnshire's preserved windmills. Built in 1813 by Oxley of Alford, it is a five-sailer owned by the County Council and often open to the public. The main road lies beyond the mill and the meadow remains unbuilt on, while the mill buildings also survive.

SKEGNESS, THE BEACH 1890 26694

This last chapter follows on geographically from where the fourth chapter finished, at Burgh le Marsh four miles west of Skegness. We are now in seaside, holiday Lincolnshire; we start in Skegness, whose skipping sailor symbol and slogan 'Skegness is so Bracing' is very well-known. Bracing is a good word to describe the north and east winds that frequently blow into the coast here, but the sand beaches are superb compensation.

SKEGNESS, THE PIER 1899 44350

Skegness owed its popular success to the railway, which reached here in 1873 as an extension from the then terminus at Wainfleet. There had been a middle-class watering place attached to what was little more than a fishing village. A new town was laid out from 1876 by the Earl of Scarbrough; in 1881 it acquired a splendid pier, seen here and unrecognisable to the modern visitor.

SKEGNESS, THE PIER 1899 44194
In 1978 the section of the pier between the concert hall at the end, from which this view was taken, was destroyed in storms. The landward end of the 1840 foot long pier had already been submerged in 1970 by the enclosed Skegness Pier Amusements, although some of the original structure can be seen at the sea end. This view shows the resort still in its genteel phase under the Earl of Scarbrough's strict control.

SKEGNESS
From the Pier 1910 62843

Skegness was very much developed with day trips and excursions in mind, utilising the railway, with influxes from the Midlands, particularly Nottingham. Here we see the funfair actually on the sands above the high water mark, including a helter-skelter tower. It was not until 1921, when the council bought the sea -front and foreshore from the Earl, that the town assumed its brasher kiss-me-quick character.

SKEGNESS, GRAND PARADE AND THE CLOCK TOWER 1899 44195
A vital landmark building in trying to relate these early views to present-day Skegness is the Jubilee Clock Tower, erected at the junction of Lumley Road with the then seafront's Grand Parade and South Parade. The Tower was built to commemorate Queen Victoria's Diamond Jubilee: this view was taken on 11 August 1899, and shows its formal opening by the Countess of Scarbrough.

SKEGNESS, THE SEAFRONT 1899 44197
The garlands from the formal opening are still evident in this view, in which visitors admire the pristine stone and brick of the Clock Tower. In the distance is the pier, a view now wholly obscured by the enormous funfair, while the front gardens to the sea front villas have long gone.

SKEGNESS
The Parade 1899

This view looks towards the Jubilee Clock Tower, with Lumley Road to its left. The buildings on the left survive, now with large shops built out at ground floor level, but the corner building on the north side of Lumley Road, to the left of the Clock Tower, has been (badly) replaced in the 1960s.

SKEGNESS
North Parade 1899

Beyond the Clock Tower the gaps were filled in by Edwardian hotels. The bracing element of Skegness is amply demonstrated by the ladies' umbrella skills in the foreground. The seafront buildings, elegant and stately, behind them have been jollified, and those on the right have a brash ground floor projection for the neon and multiple light-bulbed Casino.

SKEGNESS, THE PARADE 1899 44346

SKEGNESS, NORTH PARADE 1899 44348

SKEGNESS, GRAND PARADE 1910 62845

At this time there is a mix of motor and horse-drawn conveyances for the tripper. The villa on the left is now a modern two-storey structure, while the seafront lawns are now utterly submerged by funfair and amusements and there is little left of the sedateness shown in this view.

SKEGNESS, THE BEACH 1910 62865

The acres and acres of superb sand are what make these Lincolnshire coastal resorts such a pleasure; I remember donkey rides here, and indeed my daughters have also ridden the Skegness donkeys in the past. Here we look beyond the licensed donkey ride man, the helter-skelter and beach fun fair, the bathing machines and the booths towards the then splendid pier.

SKEGNESS, THE FIGURE EIGHT 1910 62862

Skegness's most famous fairground ride was the Figure Eight, which was regarded as a worthy rival to Coney Island! No doubt it looks tame to the present generation reared on the terrors of Alton Towers, but to a boy in the 1950s it was quite scary enough. It is now replaced by an altogether more testing version as part of the Pleasure Beach complex.

SKEGNESS, LUMLEY ROAD 1899 44192

Given the Earl of Scarbrough's family name, Lumley Road is a straight road with the old High Street winding along south of it, diverging to the left of the trees to meet again at Lumley Square in front of the railway terminus. Here we look westward from the Clock Tower, a view taken before glass-roofed arcades were added to the buildings on the right when they became shops.

SKEGNESS
Lumley Road 1899 44354
At the west end of Lumley Road there were a few shops in 1899, but the view is utterly
transformed now from Roman Bank, a reference to the old Roman sea wall.
The charmingly rustic stone lion at the left has been replaced by a corner turret and all
the buildings are now shops, many of which have been rebuilt, but the view is still
terminated by the Jubilee Clock Tower.

INGOLDMELLS, BUTLINS HOLIDAY CAMP c1955 I47024
Before you reach Ingoldmells, north of Skegness, you pass one of Butlins' largest holiday camps. Indeed, it was Billy Butlin's very first one, opened in 1936 and the first in the country. In this view we see the Art Deco theatre, now part of Fantasy Island and mutilated and virtually unrecognisable.

INGOLDMELLS, BUTLINS HOLIDAY CAMP c1955 I47026
In this view we see the rather good Art Deco 'Butlins Ingoldmells Hotel', now brutally changed. The central stone-faced pavilion has now been lowered and clad in profiled metal sheeting, while the ground floor openings have been infilled. To complete the aesthetic devastation, the whole thing has been painted pale grey except for a band of brickwork.

INGOLDMELLS, VICKERS POINT AND THE BEACH c1955 147005

Here, looking towards Ingoldmells Point, are the sandy beach and the sand dunes, a view now radically changed by the more recent sea defences with a massive concave-fronted sea wall forming a promenade. Inland, Ingoldmells is very much kiss-me-quick hat country, with vast caravan parks, amusement arcades and a fun fair whose piece de resistance is the Volcano.

CHAPEL ST LEONARDS, CHAPEL POINT c1955 C427301

To the north beyond Ingoldmells, and rather more genteel, is Chapel St Leonards, where my mother used to holiday in the 1930s. This view is taken from the sandy Roman Bank path looking to Chapel Point. The breakwaters have gone and the sea wall has been rebuilt, but most of the beach huts remain, with quaint names like Dolly's Den, Molly's and Sand Lea.

SUTTON ON SEA
The Beach 1890

Eight miles further north along the coast is Sutton on Sea, another seaside resort somewhat overshadowed by Mablethorpe, the two linked by caravan sites. The promenade seen here was built in the 1880s at a cost of £350, but it was destroyed in the catastrophic 1953 floods. The pier beside the two ladies, one with an umbrella, is all that survives; it is known as the Lion Pillar.

◆

SUTTON ON SEA
The High Street c1955

This view looks south-west along the High Street. The Bacchus Hotel, a mainly 18th-century pantiled building predating the seaside resort's expansion, survives. The late Victorian buildings opposite survive, although sadly they have had all their windows replaced, and Green's on the right is now the Park Tavern.

SUTTON ON SEA, THE BEACH 1890 26695

SUTTON ON SEA, THE HIGH STREET c1955 S235030

SANDILANDS, THE CROOKED CHURCH c1955 S480042

Sutton on Sea's parish church, St Clement's, is Lincolnshire's very own Leaning Tower of Pisa, doubtless owing to its sandy foundations having settled since it was built in 1819. There is medieval stonework in the nave, but the church is mainly 1819 brick with an 1860 chancel. The 1819 churchwardens took no chances: it was built inland, the original medieval one having been washed away by the sea.

SANDILANDS, THE VILLAGE c1955 S480023

This view is taken from the steps up to the sea wall behind the dunes, and looks across the small resort of Sandilands, just south of Sutton on Sea. In the foreground is Boathouse Cottage, now rendered, plastic-windowed and hidden behind a high rendered wall. Beyond the greenhouse is Briarwood, one of a number of rather good sub-Arts and Crafts houses dotted around Sandilands.

MABLETHORPE, THE SANDS 1890 26718

This is an archive photograph all right: few of these buildings remain, partly as a result of the tragic floods of 1953 when the sea burst through the sea walls. These have now been rebuilt as mighty ramparts, and you cannot see the sea from the streets of Mablethorpe. The resort developed after the railway arrived in 1877, although that has now gone and the motor vehicle clogs its streets.

MABLETHORPE, THE BEACH C1955 M1016

Here we see the post-1953 sea wall, stepped here to allow access to the beach. The cafe and snack bar have now been rebuilt, but the beach is as busy as ever with day trippers from Lincolnshire and further afield on any sunny weekend day.

MABLETHORPE, BUTLINS AMUSEMENT PARK C1955 M1047

The fun fair with its big wheel has been entirely replaced with a much more spectacular amusement park complex including the Dunes Theatre. A little south of this view is Queen's Park with its boating lake, but the town is not noted for its great architecture.

MABLETHORPE, MAIN STREET 1890 26717

This view, with something of a frontier town feel in 1890, is now the brashly cheery High Street. At this time, though, it is much more sedate. Dales' Lindum House and the single storey range have been rebuilt, but the buildings beyond survive: there has been much more change on the right side of the street. In the distance is the bank of the sand dunes.

MABLETHORPE, HIGH STREET c1955 M1064

In this later view, taken a little further south-west from photograph 26717, Dales' premises, Lindum House, on the corner of Wellington Road, has been rebuilt, but the former hotel beyond, now shops, can be seen. The late 1890s gabled terrace on the right survives, although somewhat crassly altered, but there has been much rebuilding beyond with amusement arcades and fun palaces.

MABLETHORPE, HIGH STREET c1955 M1038

Looking in the opposite direction, away from the coastline, our seaside resort tour peters out with busy Victorian terraces and the taller 1927 building on the right; beyond is the footbridge across the now dismantled railway, with the station yard on the right. On the left, in the open site, are now 1970s shops and a large Co-op supermarket.

Index

Alford 30, 31

Belton House 59, 60

Binbrook 26, 27

Boston 84–85, 86–87, 88, 89, 90, 91, 92

Bourne 63, 64

Branston 48

Burgh Le Marsh 97

Chapel St Leonards 109

Colsterworth 57

Coningsby 92, 93

Crowland 77, 78

Deeping St James 76, 77

Doddington 46

Donington 82, 83

Edenham 63

Gainsborough 18, 19

Grantham 50, 51, 52, 53, 54, 55, 56

Harlaxton 58

Heckington 62

Hemswell 19, 20

Holbeach 81, 82

Horncastle 35

Huttoft 30

Ingoldmells 108, 109

Lincoln 36, 37, 38–39, 40, 41, 42–43, 44, 45

Long Sutton 80

Louth 27

Ludford Magna 25, 26

Mablethorpe 112, 113, 114

Market Deeping 74, 75

Market Rasen 21, 22–23, 24

Metheringham 47

Navenby 47

Saltfleet 28

Sandilands 111

Skegness 98, 99, 100–101, 102, 103, 104, 105, 106–107

Skillington 56

Sleaford 60, 61, 62

Spalding 79, 80

Spilsby 32, 33, 34

Stamford 64, 65 66–67, 68, 69, 70–71, 72, 73

Sutton on Sea 110

Tattershall 93, 94

Tealby 24, 25

Trusthorpe 29

Waddington 48

Wainfleet All Saints 95, 96, 97

West Rasen 20

Woolsthorpe 57

Wragby 49

The Frith Book Company publishes over 100 new titles each year. A selection of those currently available are listed below. For latest catalogue please contact Frith Book Co.
Town Books 96 pages, approximately 100 photos. **County and Themed Books** 128 pages, approximately 150 photos (unless specified). All titles hardback with laminated case and jacket, except those indicated pb (paperback)

Amersham, Chesham & Rickmansworth (pb)	1-85937-340-2	£9.99	Devon (pb)	1-85937-297-x	£9.99
Andover (pb)	1-85937-292-9	£9.99	Devon Churches (pb)	1-85937-250-3	£9.99
Aylesbury (pb)	1-85937-227-9	£9.99	Dorchester (pb)	1-85937-307-0	£9.99
Barnstaple (pb)	1-85937-300-3	£9.99	Dorset (pb)	1-85937-269-4	£9.99
Basildon Living Memories (pb)	1-85937-515-4	£9.99	Dorset Coast (pb)	1-85937-299-6	£9.99
Bath (pb)	1-85937-419-0	£9.99	Dorset Living Memories (pb)	1-85937-584-7	£9.99
Bedford (pb)	1-85937-205-8	£9.99	Down the Severn (pb)	1-85937-560-x	£9.99
Bedfordshire Living Memories	1-85937-513-8	£14.99	Down The Thames (pb)	1-85937-278-3	£9.99
Belfast (pb)	1-85937-303-8	£9.99	Down the Trent	1-85937-311-9	£14.99
Berkshire (pb)	1-85937-191-4	£9.99	East Anglia (pb)	1-85937-265-1	£9.99
Berkshire Churches	1-85937-170-1	£17.99	East Grinstead (pb)	1-85937-138-8	£9.99
Berkshire Living Memories	1-85937-332-1	£14.99	East London	1-85937-080-2	£14.99
Black Country	1-85937-497-2	£12.99	East Sussex (pb)	1-85937-606-1	£9.99
Blackpool (pb)	1-85937-393-3	£9.99	Eastbourne (pb)	1-85937-399-2	£9.99
Bognor Regis (pb)	1-85937-431-x	£9.99	Edinburgh (pb)	1-85937-193-0	£8.99
Bournemouth (pb)	1-85937-545-6	£9.99	England In The 1880s	1-85937-331-3	£17.99
Bradford (pb)	1-85937-204-x	£9.99	Essex - Second Selection	1-85937-456-5	£14.99
Bridgend (pb)	1-85937-386-0	£7.99	Essex (pb)	1-85937-270-8	£9.99
Bridgwater (pb)	1-85937-305-4	£9.99	Essex Coast	1-85937-342-9	£14.99
Bridport (pb)	1-85937-327-5	£9.99	Essex Living Memories	1-85937-490-5	£14.99
Brighton (pb)	1-85937-192-2	£8.99	Exeter	1-85937-539-1	£9.99
Bristol (pb)	1-85937-264-3	£9.99	Exmoor (pb)	1-85937-608-8	£9.99
British Life A Century Ago (pb)	1-85937-213-9	£9.99	Falmouth (pb)	1-85937-594-4	£9.99
Buckinghamshire (pb)	1-85937-200-7	£9.99	Folkestone (pb)	1-85937-124-8	£9.99
Camberley (pb)	1-85937-222-8	£9.99	Frome (pb)	1-85937-317-8	£9.99
Cambridge (pb)	1-85937-422-0	£9.99	Glamorgan	1-85937-488-3	£14.99
Cambridgeshire (pb)	1-85937-420-4	£9.99	Glasgow (pb)	1-85937-190-6	£9.99
Cambridgeshire Villages	1-85937-523-5	£14.99	Glastonbury (pb)	1-85937-338-0	£7.99
Canals And Waterways (pb)	1-85937-291-0	£9.99	Gloucester (pb)	1-85937-232-5	£9.99
Canterbury Cathedral (pb)	1-85937-179-5	£9.99	Gloucestershire (pb)	1-85937-561-8	£9.99
Cardiff (pb)	1-85937-093-4	£9.99	Great Yarmouth (pb)	1-85937-426-3	£9.99
Carmarthenshire (pb)	1-85937-604-5	£9.99	Greater Manchester (pb)	1-85937-266-x	£9.99
Chelmsford (pb)	1-85937-310-0	£9.99	Guildford (pb)	1-85937-410-7	£9.99
Cheltenham (pb)	1-85937-095-0	£9.99	Hampshire (pb)	1-85937-279-1	£9.99
Cheshire (pb)	1-85937-271-6	£9.99	Harrogate (pb)	1-85937-423-9	£9.99
Chester (pb)	1-85937-382 8	£9.99	Hastings and Bexhill (pb)	1-85937-131-0	£9.99
Chesterfield (pb)	1-85937-378-x	£9.99	Heart of Lancashire (pb)	1-85937-197-3	£9.99
Chichester (pb)	1-85937-228-7	£9.99	Helston (pb)	1-85937-214-7	£9.99
Churches of East Cornwall (pb)	1-85937-249-x	£9.99	Hereford (pb)	1-85937-175-2	£9.99
Churches of Hampshire (pb)	1-85937-207-4	£9.99	Herefordshire (pb)	1-85937-567-7	£9.99
Cinque Ports & Two Ancient Towns	1-85937-492-1	£14.99	Herefordshire Living Memories	1-85937-514-6	£14.99
Colchester (pb)	1-85937-188-4	£8.99	Hertfordshire (pb)	1-85937-247-3	£9.99
Cornwall (pb)	1-85937-229-5	£9.99	Horsham (pb)	1-85937-432-8	£9.99
Cornwall Living Memories	1-85937-248-1	£14.99	Humberside (pb)	1-85937-605-3	£9.99
Cotswolds (pb)	1-85937-230-9	£9.99	Hythe, Romney Marsh, Ashford (pb)	1-85937-256-2	£9.99
Cotswolds Living Memories	1-85937-255-4	£14.99	Ipswich (pb)	1-85937-424-7	£9.99
County Durham (pb)	1-85937-398-4	£9.99	Isle of Man (pb)	1-85937-268-6	£9.99
Croydon Living Memories (pb)	1-85937-162-0	£9.99	Isle of Wight (pb)	1-85937-429-8	£9.99
Cumbria (pb)	1-85937-621-5	£9.99	Isle of Wight Living Memories	1-85937-304-6	£14.99
Derby (pb)	1-85937-367-4	£9.99	Kent (pb)	1-85937-189-2	£9.99
Derbyshire (pb)	1-85937-196-5	£9.99	Kent Living Memories(pb)	1-85937-401-8	£9.99
Derbyshire Living Memories	1-85937-330-5	£14.99	Kings Lynn (pb)	1-85937-334-8	£9.99

Available from your local bookshop or from the publisher

Frith Book Co Titles (continued)

Title	ISBN	Price	Title	ISBN	Price
Lake District (pb)	1-85937-275-9	£9.99	Sherborne (pb)	1-85937-301-1	£9.99
Lancashire Living Memories	1-85937-335-6	£14.99	Shrewsbury (pb)	1-85937-325-9	£9.99
Lancaster, Morecambe, Heysham (pb)	1-85937-233-3	£9.99	Shropshire (pb)	1-85937-326-7	£9.99
Leeds (pb)	1-85937-202-3	£9.99	Shropshire Living Memories	1-85937-643-6	£14.99
Leicester (pb)	1-85937-381-x	£9.99	Somerset	1-85937-153-1	£14.99
Leicestershire & Rutland Living Memories	1-85937-500-6	£12.99	South Devon Coast	1-85937-107-8	£14.99
Leicestershire (pb)	1-85937-185-x	£9.99	South Devon Living Memories (pb)	1-85937-609-6	£9.99
Lighthouses	1-85937-257-0	£9.99	South East London (pb)	1-85937-263-5	£9.99
Lincoln (pb)	1-85937-380-1	£9.99	South Somerset	1-85937-318-6	£14.99
Lincolnshire (pb)	1-85937-433-6	£9.99	South Wales	1-85937-519-7	£14.99
Liverpool and Merseyside (pb)	1-85937-234-1	£9.99	Southampton (pb)	1-85937-427-1	£9.99
London (pb)	1-85937-183-3	£9.99	Southend (pb)	1-85937-313-5	£9.99
London Living Memories	1-85937-454-9	£14.99	Southport (pb)	1-85937-425-5	£9.99
Ludlow (pb)	1-85937-176-0	£9.99	St Albans (pb)	1-85937-341-0	£9.99
Luton (pb)	1-85937-235-x	£9.99	St Ives (pb)	1-85937-415-8	£9.99
Maidenhead (pb)	1-85937-339-9	£9.99	Stafford Living Memories (pb)	1-85937-503-0	£9.99
Maidstone (pb)	1-85937-391-7	£9.99	Staffordshire (pb)	1-85937-308-9	£9.99
Manchester (pb)	1-85937-198-1	£9.99	Stourbridge (pb)	1-85937-530-8	£9.99
Marlborough (pb)	1-85937-336-4	£9.99	Stratford upon Avon (pb)	1-85937-388-7	£9.99
Middlesex	1-85937-158-2	£14.99	Suffolk (pb)	1-85937-221-x	£9.99
Monmouthshire	1-85937-532-4	£14.99	Suffolk Coast (pb)	1-85937-610-x	£9.99
New Forest (pb)	1-85937-390-9	£9.99	Surrey (pb)	1-85937-240-6	£9.99
Newark (pb)	1-85937-366-6	£9.99	Surrey Living Memories	1-85937-328-3	£14.99
Newport, Wales (pb)	1-85937-258-9	£9.99	Sussex (pb)	1-85937-184-1	£9.99
Newquay (pb)	1-85937-421-2	£9.99	Sutton (pb)	1-85937-337-2	£9.99
Norfolk (pb)	1-85937-195-7	£9.99	Swansea (pb)	1-85937-167-1	£9.99
Norfolk Broads	1-85937-486-7	£14.99	Taunton (pb)	1-85937-314-3	£9.99
Norfolk Living Memories (pb)	1-85937-402-6	£9.99	Tees Valley & Cleveland (pb)	1-85937-623-1	£9.99
North Buckinghamshire	1-85937-626-6	£14.99	Teignmouth (pb)	1-85937-370-4	£7.99
North Devon Living Memories	1-85937-261-9	£14.99	Thanet (pb)	1-85937-116-7	£9.99
North Hertfordshire	1-85937-547-2	£14.99	Tiverton (pb)	1-85937-178-7	£9.99
North London (pb)	1-85937-403-4	£9.99	Torbay (pb)	1-85937-597-9	£9.99
North Somerset	1-85937-302-x	£14.99	Truro (pb)	1-85937-598-7	£9.99
North Wales (pb)	1-85937-298-8	£9.99	Victorian & Edwardian Dorset	1-85937-254-6	£14.99
North Yorkshire (pb)	1-85937-236-8	£9.99	Victorian & Edwardian Kent (pb)	1-85937-624-X	£9.99
Northamptonshire Living Memories	1-85937-529-4	£14.99	Victorian & Edwardian Maritime Album (pb)	1-85937-622-3	£9.99
Northamptonshire	1-85937-150-7	£14.99	Victorian and Edwardian Sussex (pb)	1-85937-625-8	£9.99
Northumberland Tyne & Wear (pb)	1-85937-281-3	£9.99	Villages of Devon (pb)	1-85937-293-7	£9.99
Northumberland	1-85937-522-7	£14.99	Villages of Kent (pb)	1-85937-294-5	£9.99
Norwich (pb)	1-85937-194-9	£8.99	Villages of Sussex (pb)	1-85937-295-3	£9.99
Nottingham (pb)	1-85937-324-0	£9.99	Warrington (pb)	1-85937-507-3	£9.99
Nottinghamshire (pb)	1-85937-187-6	£9.99	Warwick (pb)	1-85937-518-9	£9.99
Oxford (pb)	1-85937-411-5	£9.99	Warwickshire (pb)	1-85937-203-1	£9.99
Oxfordshire (pb)	1-85937-430-1	£9.99	Welsh Castles (pb)	1-85937-322-4	£9.99
Oxfordshire Living Memories	1-85937-525-1	£14.99	West Midlands (pb)	1-85937-289-9	£9.99
Paignton (pb)	1-85937-374-7	£7.99	West Sussex (pb)	1-85937-607-x	£9.99
Peak District (pb)	1-85937-280-5	£9.99	West Yorkshire (pb)	1-85937-201-5	£9.99
Pembrokeshire	1-85937-262-7	£14.99	Weston Super Mare (pb)	1-85937-306-2	£9.99
Penzance (pb)	1-85937-595-2	£9.99	Weymouth (pb)	1-85937-209-0	£9.99
Peterborough (pb)	1-85937-219-8	£9.99	Wiltshire (pb)	1-85937-277-5	£9.99
Picturesque Harbours	1-85937-208-2	£14.99	Wiltshire Churches (pb)	1-85937-171-x	£9.99
Piers	1-85937-237-6	£17.99	Wiltshire Living Memories (pb)	1-85937-396-8	£9.99
Plymouth (pb)	1-85937-389-5	£9.99	Winchester (pb)	1-85937-428-x	£9.99
Poole & Sandbanks (pb)	1-85937-251-1	£9.99	Windsor (pb)	1-85937-333-x	£9.99
Preston (pb)	1-85937-212-0	£9.99	Wokingham & Bracknell (pb)	1-85937-329-1	£9.99
Reading (pb)	1-85937-238-4	£9.99	Woodbridge (pb)	1-85937-498-0	£9.99
Redhill to Reigate (pb)	1-85937-596-0	£9.99	Worcester (pb)	1-85937-165-5	£9.99
Ringwood (pb)	1-85937-384-4	£7.99	Worcestershire Living Memories	1-85937-489-1	£14.99
Romford (pb)	1-85937-319-4	£9.99	Worcestershire	1-85937-152-3	£14.99
Royal Tunbridge Wells (pb)	1-85937-504-9	£9.99	York (pb)	1-85937-199-x	£9.99
Salisbury (pb)	1-85937-239-2	£9.99	Yorkshire (pb)	1-85937-186-8	£9.99
Scarborough (pb)	1-85937-379-8	£9.99	Yorkshire Coastal Memories	1-85937-506-5	£14.99
Sevenoaks and Tonbridge (pb)	1-85937-392-5	£9.99	Yorkshire Dales	1-85937-502-2	£14.99
Sheffield & South Yorks (pb)	1-85937-267-8	£9.99	Yorkshire Living Memories (pb)	1-85937-397-6	£9.99

See Frith books on the internet at www.francisfrith.co.uk

FRITH PRODUCTS & SERVICES

Francis Frith would doubtless be pleased to know that the pioneering publishing venture he started in 1860 still continues today. A hundred and forty years later, The Francis Frith Collection continues in the same innovative tradition and is now one of the foremost publishers of vintage photographs in the world. Some of the current activities include:

Interior Decoration

Today Frith's photographs can be seen framed and as giant wall murals in thousands of pubs, restaurants, hotels, banks, retail stores and other public buildings throughout the country. In every case they enhance the unique local atmosphere of the places they depict and provide reminders of gentler days in an increasingly busy and frenetic world.

Product Promotions

Frith products are used by many major companies to promote the sales of their own products or to reinforce their own history and heritage. Frith promotions have been used by Hovis bread, Courage beers, Scots Porage Oats, Colman's mustard, Cadbury's foods, Mellow Birds coffee, Dunhill pipe tobacco, Guinness, and Bulmer's Cider.

Genealogy and Family History

As the interest in family history and roots grows world-wide, more and more people are turning to Frith's photographs of Great Britain for images of the towns, villages and streets where their ancestors lived; and, of course, photographs of the churches and chapels where their ancestors were christened, married and buried are an essential part of every genealogy tree and family album.

Frith Products

All Frith photographs are available Framed or just as Mounted Prints and Posters (size 23 x 16 inches). These may be ordered from the address below. From time to time other products - Address Books, Calendars, Table Mats, etc - are available.

The Internet

Already fifty thousand Frith photographs can be viewed and purchased on the internet through the Frith websites and a myriad of partner sites.

For more detailed information on Frith companies and products, look at these sites:

www.francisfrith.co.uk
www.francisfrith.com
(for North American visitors)

See the complete list of Frith Books at:

www.francisfrith.co.uk

This web site is regularly updated with the latest list of publications from the Frith Book Company. If you wish to buy books relating to another part of the country that your local bookshop does not stock, you may purchase on-line.

For further information, trade, or author enquiries please contact us at the address below:
The Francis Frith Collection, Frith's Barn, Teffont, Salisbury, Wiltshire, England SP3 5QP.
Tel: +44 (0)1722 716 376 Fax: +44 (0)1722 716 881 Email: sales@francisfrith.co.uk

See Frith books on the internet at www.francisfrith.co.uk

HOW TO ORDER YOUR FREE MOUNTED PRINT
and other Frith prints at half price

Mounted Print
Overall size 14 x 11 inches

Fill in and cut out this voucher and return it with your remittance for £2.25 (to cover postage and handling to UK addresses). For overseas addresses please include £4.00 post and handling.
Choose any photograph included in this book. Your SEPIA print will be A4 in size. It will be mounted in a cream mount with a burgundy rule line (overall size 14 x 11 inches).

Order additional Mounted Prints at HALF PRICE (only £7.49 each*)

If you would like to order more Frith prints from this book, possibly as gifts for friends and family, you can buy them at half price (with no additional postage and handling costs).

Have your Mounted Prints framed

For an extra £14.95 per print* you can have your mounted print(s) framed in an elegant polished wood and gilt moulding, overall size 16 x 13 inches (no additional postage and handling required).

---

* IMPORTANT!

These special prices are only available if you order at the same time as you order your free mounted print. You must use the ORIGINAL VOUCHER on this page (no copies permitted). We can only despatch to one address.

Voucher for **FREE** and Reduced Price Frith Prints

Please do not photocopy this voucher. Only the original is valid, so please fill it in, cut it out and return it to us with your order.

Picture ref no	Page number	Qty	Mounted @ £7.49	Framed + £14.95	Total Cost
		1	Free of charge*	£	£
			£7.49	£	£
			£7.49	£	£
			£7.49	£	£
			£7.49	£	£
			£7.49	£	£
Please allow 28 days for delivery			* Post & handling (UK)		£2.25
			Total Order Cost		£

Title of this book . . . .

I enclose a cheque/postal order for £ . . . .
made payable to 'The Francis Frith Collection'

OR please debit my Mastercard / Visa / Switch / Amex card *(credit cards please on all overseas orders),* details below

Card Number

Issue No (Switch only)   Valid from (Amex/Switch)

Expires   Signature

Name Mr/Mrs/Ms ....

Address ....
....
....
.... Postcode ....

Daytime Tel No ....

Email ....

Valid to 31/12/05

Send completed Voucher form to:
The Francis Frith Collection, Frith's Barn, Teffont, Salisbury, Wiltshire SP3 5QP

Would you like to find out more about Francis Frith?

We have recently recruited some entertaining speakers who are happy to visit local groups, clubs and societies to give an illustrated talk documenting Frith's travels and photographs. If you are a member of such a group and are interested in hosting a presentation, we would love to hear from you.

Our speakers bring with them a small selection of our local town and county books, together with sample prints. They are happy to take orders. A small proportion of the order value is donated to the group who have hosted the presentation. The talks are therefore an excellent way of fundraising for small groups and societies.

Can you help us with information about any of the Frith photographs in this book?

We are gradually compiling an historical record for each of the photographs in the Frith archive. It is always fascinating to find out the names of the people shown in the pictures, as well as insights into the shops, buildings and other features depicted.

If you recognize anyone in the photographs in this book, or if you have information not already included in the author's caption, do let us know. We would love to hear from you, and will try to publish it in future books or articles.

Our production team

Frith books are produced by a small dedicated team at offices in the converted Grade II listed 18th-century barn at Teffont near Salisbury, illustrated above. Most have worked with the Frith Collection for many years. All have in common one quality: they have a passion for the Frith Collection. The team is constantly expanding, but currently includes:

Jason Buck, John Buck, Douglas Burns, Ruth Butler, Heather Crisp, Isobel Hall, Hazel Heaton, Peter Horne, James Kinnear, Tina Leary, Sue Molloy, Hannah Marsh, Kate Rotondetto, Dean Scource, Eliza Sackett, Terence Sackett, Sandra Sanger, Lewis Taylor, and Shelley Tolcher.